W9-BYH-033

"We have the capacity, within our own heart and awareness, to handle panic attacks. *Calming the Rush of Panic* is a clear and compassionate guide in navigating this acute form of fear. Through wise teachings, case studies and a range of reflections and meditations, this book will strengthen your inner resources and nourish your spirit."

> —Tara Brach, PhD, author of *Radical Acceptance*
> and *True Refuge*

"An extremely useful and practical book that goes to the very heart of the matter. If you wholeheartedly embody in practice what it recommends, it can help transform a tendency to panic into an opening to greater balance of mind, self-acceptance, and self-compassion, right in that moment. Ultimately, it manifests as wisdom. That is the power of mindfulness. And it is already yours."

> — Jon Kabat-Zinn, author of *Full Catastrophe Living*
> and *Mindfulness for Beginners*

"Panic attacks are one-two punches: they feel dreadful, plus people shrink their lives to avoid having another one. With kindness, insight, and research-proven methods, this book shows you how to prevent panic attacks or ride them out with less suffering, plus how to reclaim your own full life. Grounded in the power of mindfulness, full of effective tools and practices, and rich with the authors' warmth and genuine wisdom, this is a remarkable guide to a life beyond panic."

> —Rick Hanson, PhD, author of *Buddha's Brain* and
> *Just One Thing*

"In addition to the clearly presented instructions for counteracting and overcoming panic, what makes this book special is the uniformly kind tone of voice of these authors throughout. They embody the wisdom of health professionals in emergency situations: they reassure, and they convey confidence and hope. You believe that they are teaching out of personal experience!"

—Sylvia Boorstein, author of *Happiness Is an Inside Job*

"Delightfully clear and practical, *Calming the Rush of Panic* offers profound insights from ancient wisdom traditions and modern psychology to help free oneself from panic attacks and live a healthier, more joyful life. The mindfulness practices offered are wise, scientific, nourishing, and transformative. Grounded in modern science, yet written from the heart, this book is a gem."

—Shauna L. Shapiro, associate professor at Santa Clara University, clinical psychologist, and coauthor of *The Art and Science of Mindfulness*

"Grounded in the experiential and direct, this pragmatic approach will help you become intimate with the taste, touch, and 'mind' of fear. Of course, no one wants to look closely at such painful experiences. Yet, deftly guided by the authors into developing a clear-minded relationship with the unwanted, you'll learn to catalyze within yourself the openness, kindness, clarity, and love that have the power to liberate and release you from the knot of panic."

—Saki Santorelli, EdD, MA, associate professor of medicine at Massachusetts Medical School and author of *Heal Thy Self*

calming
the rush
of panic

A MINDFULNESS-BASED STRESS REDUCTION GUIDE

to freeing yourself from panic attacks
& living a vital life

BOB STAHL, PhD
WENDY MILLSTINE

New Harbinger Publications, Inc.

Publisher's Note

This publication is designed to provide accurate and authoritative information in regard to the subject matter covered. It is sold with the understanding that the publisher is not engaged in rendering psychological, financial, legal, or other professional services. If expert assistance or counseling is needed, the services of a competent professional should be sought.

Distributed in Canada by Raincoast Books

Copyright © 2013 by Bob Stahl and Wendy Millsine
New Harbinger Publications, Inc.
5674 Shattuck Avenue
Oakland, CA 94609
www.newharbinger.com

"Allow" by Danna Faulds. Used by permission of the author.

"Unconditional" from POEMS FOR THE PATH by Jennifer Paine Welwood, copyright © 1988 by Jennifer Paine Welwood, and used by permission.

Copyright © 1998 by Wendell Berry from *The Selected Poems of Wendell Berry*. Reprinted by permission of Counterpoint.

Cover design by Amy Shoup; Acquired by Tesilya Hanauer; Edited by Will DeRooy

All Rights Reserved

Library of Congress Cataloging in Publication Data

Stahl, Bob.
  Calming the rush of panic : a mindfulness-based stress reduction guide to freeing yourself from panic attacks and living a vital life / Bob Stahl, Phd, Wendy Millstine.
       pages cm
  Summary: "Written by Bob Stahl, coauthor of the bestselling book, Mindfulness-Based Stress Reduction Workbook, Calming the Rush of Panic offers readers powerful mindfulness-based stress reduction (MBSR) practices in a quick, accessible format to help them cope with panic disorder. The book contains guided mindfulness meditations and exercises to help reduce fears, restore feelings of security and safety, stay calm, and get back to living life"-- Provided by publisher.
  Includes bibliographical references.
   ISBN 978-1-60882-526-4 (pbk.) -- ISBN 978-1-60882-527-1 (PDF e-book) -- ISBN 978-1-60882-528-8 (ePub) 1. Panic attacks--Popular works. 2. Stress management--Popular works. 3. Self-help techniques. I. Millstine, Wendy, 1966- II. Title.
  RC535.S72 2013
  616.85'223--dc23

                                            2012034636

Printed in the United States of America

15   14   13

10   9   8   7   6   5   4   3 · 2   1   First printing

I dedicate this book to all who embrace their panic, fear, or anxiety and open to healing and peace. May we all find the gateways into our hearts and grow in wisdom and compassion.

Bob Stahl

This book is dedicated to all those who struggle with panic attacks. May it help you find deep compassion for and loving acceptance of yourself, and may you find healing and happiness along the way. It is also dedicated to N., who taught me how to fly with my heart wide open, trust myself, and experience life and love to the fullest.

Wendy Millstine

Contents

Acknowledgments. ix

Introduction. 1

Fear   2
Panic   3
Anxiety   4
The Basis of Our Approach   4
Overview of the Book   5
About Us, the Authors   8

Foundation. 13

The Many Causes of Panic   14
How Mindfulness Helps   14
MBSR   15
Mindfulness Attitudes   17
Establishing a Formal Practice of Mindfulness: Meditation   19
Establishing an Informal Practice of Mindfulness: Mindfulness in Daily Activities   25

1   Calming the Rush of Panic in Your Body 29

Mindful Breathing   30
    Foundational Practice: Mindful Breathing   31
The Body Scan   35
    Foundational Practice: The Body Scan   36

S.T.O.P.   43
Applied Practices   46
   Kick Off a Good Day   47
   Start Your Morning with Mindfulness   49
   Wash Away Your Panic   52
   Drive with More Ease   54
   Give a Worry-Free Presentation   57
   Get Grounded   59
   Find Balance   61
   Get a Good Night's Rest   63
Here We Are   65

2 Calming the Rush of Panic in Your Emotions and Feelings. 67
Mindful Inquiry   68
   Foundational Practice: Mindful Inquiry   74
R.A.I.N.   76
Applied Practices   79
   Start Your Morning Off Right   80
   Restore Peace in Your Heart   83
   A Good Day's Work   86
   Transform Your Anger   88
   Free Yourself from Feeling Out of Control   91
   Work Through Painful Emotions   94
   Let Emotions Be   97
   Get the Rest You Need   100
Here We Are   102

3 Calming the Rush of Panic in Your Thoughts . 103
Sitting Meditation   104
   Foundational Practice: Sitting Meditation   111
Pause, Observe/Experience, and Allow   116
Applied Practices   120
   Relax about Social Situations   121

Overcome Your Fear of Crowds or Tight Spaces   124
Cope with Your Fear of Illness   127
Dissipate All-Consuming Thoughts   130
Calm Your Fear of Being Alone   133
Find Freedom from Thoughts of Death   135
Quiet Your Fears of the Unknown   138
Feel Comfortable around Others   141
Here We Are   143

4   Life Beyond Panic. 145
Loving-Kindness Meditation   147
    Foundational Practice: Loving-Kindness Meditation   148
The Web of Life   153
    Foundational Practice: The "Web of Life" Meditation   155
Applied Practices   158
    Contentment   159
    Self-Love and Appreciation   161
    The Gift of Panic   164
    Balance and Joy   167
    Compassion   170
    Sacredness   173
    Happiness and Love   176
    Interconnectedness   179
Supporting Your Practice   181
Closing Words   183

Resources 187

References 193

Acknowledgments

To my co-author, Wendy Millstine—who approached me with the idea for this book and contributed all the applied practices—my deepest thanks. I have appreciated your dear and wise heart.

To Taungpulu Sayadaw, Hlaing Tet Sayadaw, Pakokku Sayadaw, and Dr. Rina Sircar—my teachers—without you, I would not be on this mindful and heartfelt path. I am also deeply indebted to my parents, Marilyn and Alvan; my beloved wife, Jan; and our two sons, Ben and Bodhi, whose love and support means the world to me.

To my dear friends Jon Kabat-Zinn, Saki Santorelli, Florence Melio-Meyer, and Melissa Blacker—all masterful MBSR teachers who live with wise and open hearts and inspire me deeply—I am deeply grateful. Much appreciation to my dear dhamma friends who have nurtured me along the way: Mary Grace Orr, Steve Flowers, Karen Zelin, Bruce Eisendorf, Ed Plonka, Dan Landry, Jill and Bruce Hyman, Jason Murphy, Marcy Reynolds, and Skip Regan. Lastly, I am deeply grateful and indebted to all my students, from whom I have learned so much.

Bob Stahl

With deep gratitude, we would like to thank the following people who have dedicated their lives to the alleviation of suffering, panic, and pain, and who have endorsed our book: Tara Brach, Jon Kabat-Zinn, Sylvia Boorstein, Saki Santorelli, Shauna Shapiro, and Rick Hanson. We would also like to thank New Harbinger Publications for supporting this book, as well as Tesilya Hanauer and Jess Beebe, who were our editors, and Will DeRooy, our copy editor. We thank them deeply for their thoughtfulness and skill in the development of this book as well as the wonderful wordsmithing.

Bob and Wendy

Introduction

Have you ever been about to give a speech or ask someone out on a date and found yourself forgetting what you were going to say, sweating, feeling nauseated, or trembling? Maybe your heart started pounding and you felt short of breath, dizzy, disorientated, or numb. If these sensations caused you to worry that you might go crazy, lose control, or even actually die of fright, you most likely have had a panic attack. Panic is an extreme reaction to being in a fearful situation. It can be paralyzing or can make you feel out of control.

If you experience panic from time to time, you're not alone. In fact, more people live with panic than you might imagine. Many people don't like to talk about their feelings of panic or even admit to themselves how panic affects and limits their lives. We live in a culture that often denies or avoids admitting that we live with panic, anxiety, or even fear.

Although "fear," "panic," and "anxiety" are commonly used interchangeably, in psychology they refer to separate experiences. Let's look briefly at each of these terms.

Fear

Fear is a natural and direct response to anything you perceive as an immediate threat to your safety. Humans and many other creatures are "hardwired" to feel fear. That is to say, fear and your immediate reaction to it are governed by a primitive part of the brain that is not under your conscious control. When you're faced with immediate danger, fear serves to activate your "fight, flight, or freeze" response in order to help you survive. This response engages one of the two opposite components of your *autonomic* (self-directed) *nervous system*. When you take action against a threat by fighting or fleeing, your *sympathetic nervous system* kicks in. It "puts the pedal to the metal," igniting physical changes such as increased heart rate, spiked blood pressure, rapid breathing, and the release of endorphins to numb pain. At the same time, bodily functions less crucial to your immediate survival, such as digestion, immune function, and reproductive function, slow down or temporarily come to a stop. This kind of response can lend you seemingly superhuman ability, of the sort that enables a mother to pick up the back of a car that has pinned her child down. On the other hand, when the primitive part of your brain judges that a situation is hopeless—that no action will help—it activates your *parasympathetic nervous system*, much like slamming on the brakes. This creates the freeze response; it lowers blood pressure and heart rate to aid in immobilizing the body and storing energy for a time when it might be put to better use.

Fear is instinctual, an artifact of evolution that has been with us for ages. It's an inescapable part of life.

Panic

Panic is like an allergic reaction to fear. Panic affects your body, emotions, and thoughts in extreme ways and can feel like a violent eruption. To help illustrate this point, if you walk too close to the edge of a cliff, your fear response may kick in, prompting you to jump back to a safe distance. With panic, however, when you see the edge of that cliff, your skin may tingle, you may feel hot and sweaty, or you may feel cold and shiver. Your heart rate and respiration rate may increase sharply, or your stomach may feel queasy or tight. Your jaw may clench, or your muscles may tie themselves in knots. You may feel as if you're trapped, and your emotions and thoughts may run wild, telling you that you have to escape. Your mind can become filled with stories of terror, worry, anger, shame, inadequacy, or embarrassment or with fears that you're going crazy or dying. You may grow hysterical and irrational. You may try to bargain, plead, or beg for these feelings to go away. Alternatively, your mind may go blank and you may freeze in your tracks. Whatever your reaction, you may later try to avoid cliffs (or similar situations) even more, for fear of experiencing these feelings again.

Anxiety

Anxiety is mostly associated with worrying about possible future threats. For example, perhaps you worry about getting too close to the edges of cliffs even when you're not in the vicinity of a cliff. Anxious thoughts can be accompanied by physiological symptoms such as musculoskeletal tension, insomnia, loss of (or increase in) appetite, or nausea. Anxious feelings can at times lead to a panic attack, especially if you're imagining a worst-case scenario like falling off a cliff.

We also want to acknowledge that their are many types of anxiety disorders, including social and generalized anxiety, post-traumatic stress, agoraphobia, and other phobias such as fear of spiders and fear of flying.

The Basis of Our Approach

This book will teach you perspectives and methods from *mindfulness-based stress reduction* (MBSR) for alleviating your panic. Mindfulness is the practice of living in the here and now, with nonjudgmental awareness and with your full attention on whatever you're currently doing or experiencing. Developed by Jon Kabat-Zinn at the University of Massachusetts Medical Center in 1979, MBSR has been proven to help people with panic and anxiety disorders, as documented in medical journals. Research has shown that MBSR techniques have long-term benefits: in one study, even three years after learning how to do mindfulness meditation—in which you simply notice your sensations, feelings, and thoughts, without judging or getting caught up in them—many people still managed their panic and anxiety much better than before (Miller, Fletcher, and Kabat-Zinn 1993).

While it's natural to feel fear when you face a situation that you're not confident you can handle, panic may, ironically, keep you from responding as competently as you might. If you can use mindfulness to focus your attention and maintain your faculties, you can work through the feelings of fear so you don't panic or, if you do panic, you can get through the situation more smoothly. When you view your experience of fear from a matter-of-fact and nonjudgmental perspective, you have the opportunity to respond more skillfully rather than from old reactive patterns that could lead to more angst and distress.

Overview of the Book

We first lay out a foundation of mindfulness that incorporates how important mindfulness attitudes can temper panic. We explain the meaning of "formal practice of mindfulness" and "informal practice of mindfulness." We also talk about how to deal with (or "work with") common challenges as you establish and carry out your own formal practice of mindfulness.

After that, in chapters 1 to 3 we look in turn at the body, emotions and feelings, and thoughts. Each of these chapters provides background, foundational (formal) practices, other (more informal) practices, and eight hands-on ("applied") practices, to help you put concepts into action and cement your practice of mindfulness.

In the last chapter, we look at life beyond panic, pointing out that as you grow in mindfulness and loving-kindness you'll begin to experience more of the interconnectedness of life and live with less panic.

In this book you'll learn four mindfulness meditations that are part of the foundation of MBSR: mindful breathing, the body scan, sitting meditation, and loving-kindness meditation. You'll also learn other ways to strengthen your practice of mindfulness, such as mindful inquiry and the "web of life" meditation, and the S.T.O.P., R.A.I.N., and "Pause, Observe/ Experience, and Allow" practices, which you can use in any situation that might lead you to panic.

Last, in each chapter you will also read stories of people who learned how to work with and transform their panic. The people in these stories are composites of some actual people we have worked with.

Chapter 1: Calming the Rush of Panic in Your Body

This chapter focuses on the physical symptoms commonly associated with panic, whether you experience these symptoms when you give a speech, get stuck in an elevator, or do anything you are uncomfortable with. We introduce you to two essentials of MBSR—mindful breathing and the body scan—as well as the MBSR mindful practice of S.T.O.P. as a way you can deal with panicky body sensations in specific situations.

Chapter 2: Calming the Rush of Panic in Your Emotions and Feelings

In this chapter, we look at emotions and feelings commonly associated with panic, such as worry, embarrassment, shame, unworthiness, inadequacy, and feelings of impending doom or going crazy. We introduce you to mindful inquiry meditation and the mindful practice R.A.I.N. as ways to lessen your emotional suffering and to foster a deeper sense of ease and balance.

Chapter 3: Calming the Rush of Panic in Your Thoughts

In this chapter, we explore how thoughts fuel panic through rumination, anticipation of future panic attacks, "what if" thinking, and habitual thought patterns. We examine how fearful thoughts related to illness, aging, death, the unknown, being alone, being in crowds, being in enclosed spaces, or being away from home can foster ongoing panic, as can thoughts of people, animals, or situations that make you feel uncomfortable. There are countless ways that panic can manifest. You'll learn sitting meditation—another fundamental constituent of MBSR—as a way to recognize that thoughts are just thoughts: your thoughts are not necessarily "true," nor are they the totality of you. It may be liberating to realize that you are not your thoughts—that they are not a complete definition of who you are. You'll also learn "Pause, Observe/Experience, and Allow" as a way to manage your panic.

Chapter 4: Life beyond Panic

This last chapter is an exploration of how to connect to the essence of life beyond the immediate physical and emotional experiences of panic. How can the experience of panic also be an opportunity for deeper awareness and discovery? You'll learn loving-kindness meditation, as well as the "web of life" meditation, and deepen your experience of the interconnectedness of life through applied practices. You'll learn how to transform your panic to bring you closer to what's most important, such as family, love, happiness, abundance, and the simple things in life.

We want to affirm that you have immense resources for healing and well-being within you. There's no need to look outside of yourself—everything you need to know is already inside. You simply need to access it. It begins right here, in this moment. This sentiment is captured beautifully in the *Tao Te Ching* by Lao-tzu (1944, 55):

> There is no need to run outside
> For better seeing,
> Nor to peer from a window. Rather abide
> At the center of your being;
> For the more you leave it, the less you learn.
> Search your heart and see
> If he is wise who takes each turn:
> The way to do is to be.

About Us, the Authors

Bob Stahl

My interest in panic is very personal. It began at the age of four when I first realized the truth of death, which none of us can escape. It was shocking to apprehend that I and everyone else was going to die and that it could happen at any moment. That first realization left me almost out of breath and stunned. If that wasn't a powerful enough teaching, in the next few years I lost my brother, grandfather, and best friend. This left me in a state of desperation, grief, and at times panic over what I was going to do with this life and how I should live if it all ended with death. I spent a lot of time pondering the meaning of life.

I grew up in Boston, in the turbulent 1960s, when the times they were a-changing. Like many young people in my generation, I experimented with powerful mind-altering drugs, starting in high school. On one such occasion I was made fun of and humiliated by some of my so-called friends. I became panicked and frightened, so much that I lost touch with reality and felt as though I was going to either go mad or die. As a result of feeling out of control in this unsafe emotional environment, I experienced tremendous panic in my body, emotions, and thoughts. After that experience, I underwent panic attacks nearly every day for months and thought I was truly going to lose myself, go completely crazy, or die. That year of school my grades plummeted from A's and B's to D's and F's.

Feeling lost, scared, and pretty hopeless, I turned to my parents and shared with them what was happening to me. With their support, I started seeing a wonderful psychiatrist who helped me find my way back to myself. I began to learn to slowly face my fears and panic by acknowledging the physical feelings along with my emotions and thoughts instead of running away from them. At first this felt counterintuitive, just like turning the steering wheel of a car in the direction of the skid when you begin to lose control on a snowy or icy road. But lo and behold, as I turned toward my fears and panic, they began to subside and I straightened out. In actuality, they not only dissipated, but in time, as I developed deeper insight and understanding into what was fueling them, I began to feel more and more freedom—more than I had ever imagined was possible.

Mindfulness has truly transformed my life, and I trust it will do the same for you. I believe that there's no special starting point other than the intention to begin right now. No matter how panic-laced, hopeless, unworthy, or inadequate you may feel, there's hope for you. The path of mindfulness and the heart is open to all—no matter who you are or what you've done. Let's take this first step that is upon us right here and now.

Wendy Millstine

My first panic attack occurred soon after my thirteen-year marriage ended. The person I had come to believe was my life partner and soul companion was walking out the door, resolute in his decision to leave our marriage for someone else. Then the painful triggers began. For me, a trigger might come in the form of a thought, an emotion, or a physical sensation. The thought of bearing the label "divorcée" felt akin to being a widow. On these occasions, I found myself obsessing over these thoughts like a hamster in a wheel. *Why me? Why me? Why me?...* My feelings at this utter betrayal swung between anger and the darkest sadness that I had ever come to know. Frequently all it took was an e-mail from my ex-husband or an envelope addressed to both of us to make me feel as though I couldn't breathe. My heart would start pounding painfully in my throat, then I would feel nauseated, and I'd be forced to leave work and race home for safety.

I tried many different healing paths for coping with my panic issues—exercising, eating healthy, enrolling in school, focusing on my art and writing projects, traveling—but nothing quite settled my panic attacks until I started practicing mindfulness meditation, considered by some to be the Buddha's enlightened path to end suffering. Mindfulness is simply the conscious act of paying attention to whatever you're experiencing, moment by moment, without judgment. I discovered that the power of being in the now—in this exact present moment, breath by breath—actually changed my relationship to my experience of panic. Over time, my practice of mindfulness became an opportunity to experience panic in a new way. In fact, when I turned toward and tuned in to my panic, I felt it dissipate.

My informal practice of mindfulness gives me time to sort through my reactions and time to moderate my response. My daily, formal practice of mindfulness helped me discover that if I firmly root myself in my core values—love, respect, compassion, gratitude, and helping others—I can come to know myself in deeper ways, ways outside my panic-identified self. Being mindful of my panicky thoughts, feelings, and sensations allows me a profound empathy and understanding for myself and others. And I feel less alone in my suffering.

Many of the mindful practices in this book are based on my direct experience and understanding of panic. I've personally used these practices daily and shared them with others. This book will teach you how this moment, right now, is a gift. The practice of being present with yourself can change how you relate and respond to your panic, which in turn will help you manage your panic. Following in the path of the Buddha, mindfulness meditations are a prescription for hope and courage for a life beyond panic. Allow us to be your gentle guides on this journey.

Foundation

Mindfulness, which comes to us from early Buddhist meditative disciplines, consists most importantly of bringing your awareness into the present moment. Mindfulness has been mainstreamed into various mindfulness-based interventions and research in medicine, science, psychology, education, and business. Mindfulness is present-moment nonjudgmental awareness; you can imagine mindfulness as similar to a meteorologist who reports the weather just as it is.

When you begin to observe the workings of your mind, as we guide you to do in this book, you may realize that you're often not present—that you're "somewhere else" mentally—generally either rehearsing the future or rehashing the past. But consider this: the only moment you ever live in is right now, so why not be here? Mindfulness is never beyond your reach; it's as close as your conscious attention. The moment you realize you're not present, you are in fact present.

The Many Causes of Panic

As stated, research has demonstrated that mindfulness-based stress reduction can be extremely beneficial in decreasing panic. We're sure that you too can use these mindful practices to live better with panic and decrease the challenges you face.

Before you get started, you should know that although most cases of panic stem from the psyche, there are some cases in which it derives from physiological sources. Although mindfulness training may help you regardless of the cause of your panic, you may also need to consult a health care professional to investigate whether there's any biological reason you feel panicky. In addition, if your panic attacks are frequent or severe, it's best if you take steps to address your panic under the guidance and supervision of a health care professional.

Sometimes a very active thyroid (hyperthyroidism), low blood sugar (hypoglycemia), heart arrhythmia, or other physiological conditions can lead you to panic. Some medications and herbs may have side effects that make you susceptible to panic. You may also want to look at diet as a contributing factor, especially if you consume lots of caffeine or highly refined carbs and sugary foods.

How Mindfulness Helps

Let's find out now about how mindfulness can improve your health and well-being. As stated, practicing mindfulness has been shown to decrease panic and anxiety. There are numerous studies illustrating that mindfulness has a wide range of other benefits, too. It can help decrease chronic pain, increase stress hardiness and resilience, reduce psoriasis symptoms, and improve immune system function (Center for Mindfulness in Medicine, Health Care, and Society n.d.).

Some astounding studies have also shown positive changes in dealing with stress as seen through functional magnetic resonance imaging (FMRI) of the brain's structure and function. These studies (Davidson et al. 2003; Hölzel et al. 2011) show that the way people intentionally shape their internal focus of attention induces a state of brain activation during their mindfulness meditation that increases resiliency and positive responses to stress. It's said that "neurons that fire together, wire together," meaning that with repetition, an intentionally created state can become an enduring trait of the individual as reflected in long-term changes in brain function and structure. This is a fundamental property of *neuroplasticity*—how the brain changes in response to experience. These are just a few of the many studies that show that mindfulness can play an extremely important role on health through cultivating the mind.

MBSR

Mindfulness-based stress reduction (MBSR) was developed by Jon Kabat-Zinn, PhD, at the University of Massachusetts Medical Center in 1979. As of this writing, there are now more than 450 MBSR programs in the United States alone, and they can be found on every continent of the world. Mindfulness can be considered a way of life that can be practiced both formally and informally, in ways that support one another. The heart of MBSR is the practice of mindfulness.

A formal practice of mindfulness (which is fully described below) usually involves regular use of the following: mindful breathing, the body scan, sitting meditation, loving-kindness meditation, and mindful movement (yoga and walking meditation). In this book we introduce you to most of these meditations as well as to some others, such as mindful inquiry and the "web of life" meditation. An informal practice of mindfulness involves bringing mindfulness into the various activities of daily living, such as cooking, eating, bathing, washing the dishes, folding laundry, and conversing. In this book we also offer some other applications of mindfulness.

Bringing together formal and informal practice of mindfulness forms a way of being in life that's more present and attentive. You begin to see more clearly where you are, how you're feeling, and how you can respond more constructively to fear and panic, anger, sadness, or whatever you may be feeling.

Mindfulness creates a space between you and what you're experiencing so you can choose how you respond. Stephen Covey (2008, viii) reiterates this powerful insight and possibility: "Between stimulus and response, there is a space. In that space lies our freedom and our power to choose our response. In our response lies our growth and our happiness."

When you react in ways that aren't mindful, they can gradually grow into habits that are detrimental to your health and well-being. Consequently, these patterns of reactivity further your suffering or distress. This is why it's so important to discern clearly the difference between reacting with unawareness and responding with mindfulness. When you become aware of the present moment, you gain access to resources you may not have had before. You may not be able to change a situation, but you can mindfully change your response to it. You can choose a more constructive and productive way of dealing with stress rather than a counterproductive or even destructive way of dealing with it.

In regard to panic, when you become mindful that you are in a state of panic, you can begin to respond to it in a way that lessens its intensity rather than inflaming or fueling it. As your practice of mindfulness deepens, you can gradually prevent panic attacks from even occurring and begin to feel much more deeply at ease within yourself and in the world.

Mindfulness Attitudes

Cultivating mindfulness begins with developing and maintaining some central attitudes. These attitudes are interrelated and support one another. See whether you can bring these attitudes into your life and into your formal practice of mindfulness as you read this book. They play an important part in the meditations and other practices we describe.

Intention is an important attitude that supports all the ones below. Establishing your intention is a powerful element in healing. When you establish your intention, you begin to believe in yourself and your own internal capacities or resources for healing. You realize that the answers are within you and not outside of you. Your intention sets you on the path to support and nurture all other attitudes to help you overcome panic and to live with more ease in your body and mind.

Beginner's mind is specifically about experiencing everything as if for the first time, seeing things as if they were fresh and new.

In other words, beginner's mind entails being curious and letting go of the idea that you already know all about something. When you experience panic, you're usually preoccupied with thoughts of what's going to happen. This fear of the future supersedes what's actually happening in the present. For that reason, you should try to cultivate a spirit of investigation into panic.

Nonjudgment involves recognizing what's happening in the moment without judgment. When you judge your thoughts and feelings, you take yourself out of the present moment because you're no longer focusing on what you're thinking or feeling; you're focusing on your interpretations. A nonjudgmental attitude toward panic would mean thinking simply, *Oh, this is panic*, without adding anything further, when you felt the symptoms of panic. As an analogy, again, think of a meteorologist who reports the weather just as it is.

The following three attitudes—nonstriving, allowing, and letting be—may seem similar, yet each offers subtly different ways of helping you deal with panic with greater precision and clarity in your mindful approach.

Nonstriving is an attitude of not trying, striving, or attempting to achieve anything. In regard to panic, this means a willingness to be with things as they are. As you embrace nonstriving, your panic will gradually lessen because your energy isn't spent trying to fight or resist it.

Allowing means acknowledging what's present for you. Rather than trying to push away panic, you allow yourself to experience it. An allowing attitude gives space to your experience of panic—just like the sky gives space for a storm to pass through and by that virtue it eventually dissipates.

Letting be is an attitude of not trying to change your experience. In regard to dealing with panic, you let the panic be, not trying to let it go or trying to get rid of it. You let the panic take its own course, knowing that "this, too, will pass."

Self-reliance is a trust in your own direct experience of your life. What this means is that you realize that you possess the inner resources to understand your panic and transform it into greater ease of being.

Balance or equanimity is an understanding attitude that embraces the fact that all things change. Equanimity generally means steadiness or evenness of mind. As your understanding of impermanence grows, you can live with more balance and have a broader perspective. You can learn to "go with the flow" of life, even during a panic attack, rather than putting all your energy into fighting it. This will support you in feeling more at ease with the way things are.

Self-compassion involves regarding yourself with kindheartedness. When you have self-compassion, you realize that your greatest adversary is your own critical and judgmental self. At the same time, you forgive yourself for judging yourself and others.

Establishing a Formal Practice of Mindfulness: Meditation

As mentioned, mindfulness is a way of life that's practiced in two interrelated ways: through formal and informal practice. To truly integrate mindfulness into your life, it's important that you do both types of practice. Each complements the other. Use them every day to reduce panic and live with more ease in your body and mind.

The cultivation of a formal practice of mindfulness begins with setting an intention and deciding on a time to do it. Try to prioritize this time for your own self-care. You deserve this, and it's truly a gift to yourself that no one else can give you. Find a place that's quiet and comfortable, at a time during the day when you won't be interrupted. Turn off your phone and any other devices, and let your family know you're going to be quiet and meditate for a while; ask that you not be disturbed.

The best time to formally practice mindfulness is whenever you can do it. Some people like to practice before they get out of bed. Others like to practice after their morning stretches. Others practice during their lunch hour or in the afternoon. Many have found it helpful to practice after coming home from work or after dinner. Some even practice before they go to sleep. Find a time that works for you and let your practice grow.

Once you find a time that works, try to practice daily, even if you don't really feel like it. We suggest thirty minutes for many of the meditations, although you can practice them for shorter periods of time if need be. Even five minutes of practice is better than none at all. If your formal practice of mindfulness is spotty, don't beat yourself up or give up on it. Remember to treat yourself with kindness and compassion, and encourage yourself as you would a friend.

In this book you'll learn the formal mindful practices of mindful breathing, the body scan, mindful inquiry meditation, sitting meditation, loving-kindness meditation, and the "web of life" meditation as meaningful and direct ways to deal with panic.

Posture

Even though a formal practice of mindfulness essentially consists of meditation, you don't have to assume the stereotypical lotus position, hands on knees with palms upward and thumbs and index fingers touching. In fact, the only recommendation for posture during your practice is that you find a position in which you can be comfortable and fully alert. Some people prefer to sit in a chair or on a cushion on the floor, while others like to lie down or even stand. Any position is fine so long as you can maintain a good degree of comfort and attention.

If you take a sitting position on a cushion or chair, try to keep your back reasonably straight; don't slouch. An upright posture supports wakefulness. Try to find a good balance between comfort and alertness, making small adjustments as necessary, as if you were tuning an instrument.

If you choose to lie down, you'll need to be diligent in maintaining your awareness so that you don't fall asleep. You can keep your eyes partially open if that helps. If you still find yourself nodding off, feel free to stand up. Standing meditation is a wonderful way to practice and one way to make sure you won't fall asleep. Just stand in one place, preferably not leaning on anything, and attend to your practice. If you get tired from standing and you need to change your position, you may do so mindfully.

How to Deal with Challenges

When you formally practice mindfulness, from time to time you'll experience challenges that are considered hindrances for your growing practice. You may wonder why you'd want to bring awareness to your panic in the first place, because all you've ever wanted is to get away from it. You may even have fears that your panic could get worse if you pay attention to it. Although it's normal to feel this way, you may be surprised to discover that as you gradually turn toward panic with greater awareness, acknowledgment, and compassion, it will subside—just as turning in the direction of the skid straightens you out on a snowy or icy road. Even though it feels counterintuitive at first, the seeds of possibility are there if you're open to them.

Let's look at other predictable challenges that will arise when you practice mindfulness. When you begin to meditate, you'll soon notice how frequently your mind wanders or is consumed with wanting, avoiding, restlessness, sleepiness, or doubt.

Wandering Mind

One of the first insights you'll experience when you first begin a formal practice of mindfulness is how busy your mind is and how much it wanders. Rest assured that it's always been that way—you've just never been very mindful of its activity. Although you may think that an inability to focus means you're no good at meditating, most everyone's mind inevitably wanders during meditation. It can even be helpful to notice your mind's activity when it becomes distracted. You may discover that your thoughts and emotions are often preoccupied with either rehearsing the future or rehashing the past. This insight into the workings of your mind will give you important information. You may realize, for example, that you need to deal with an unresolved relationship or other unfinished business.

In dealing with your wandering mind, you'll begin to understand more about your mind-body connection. When you come back to the present moment after wandering off with various worries, you may notice that your jaw is clenched or your stomach is in knots. You'll begin to realize that these physical tensions are connected to your thoughts and emotions.

Another use for the wandering mind is concentration training. The way to build and sustain concentration is to repeatedly bring your mind back to the present after it has wandered off. Just like lifting weights again and again to grow muscle, when you bring your mind back again and again to your breathing or whatever you're meditating on, you increase your capacity for attention.

As your practice of mindfulness deepens, you'll understand that (a) the only changes you can ever make are in the here and now and (b) the moment you realize you're not present, you are in fact present. This is "where the rubber meets the road," starting in this moment.

Wanting or Avoiding

In addition to your mind's wanderings, you'll also be swept away at times with wanting things that make you feel good or trying to avoid things that don't. Wanting and avoiding are opposite sides of the same coin, because both are concerned with a state of feeling good. The antidote is to know when it's happening—when you're getting tangled up in a state of wanting or avoiding. This knowing helps you see where you are, and then and only then can you begin to untangle yourself.

Restlessness or Sleepiness

Restlessness and sleepiness are also opposite sides of the same coin, because at the heart of each is a desire to escape the present moment. Restlessness is like a pacing tiger that cannot be in his or her own skin, and sleepiness is filled with sloth and torpor and not being able to stay awake. Both of these challenges can keep you from being present to the workings of your body and mind with the desire to either get away from the discomfort or go to sleep and not be present. Once again, the antidote is your knowing mind. Once you *know* that you're restless or sleepy, you can begin to choose how you're going to respond to it. Restlessness is unharnessed energy that, when accessed, can be of great support to you. With sleepiness, you may want to intensify your practice in order to bring more wakefulness. You may need to open your eyes, change your posture, and splash a few drops of cold water on your face, particularly if you're often falling asleep or numbing out. If all else fails, sleep and be happy, and when you wake up, begin your practice again.

Doubt

The last challenge is being filled with doubt. You may think, *This meditation is not going to help me. What's the use? I'm never going to diminish my panicky feelings and feel better.* The antidote for doubt is *awareness,* similar to the other hindrances. When you *know* that you're experiencing doubt, you can begin to deal with it. Doubt is something to be acknowledged just like any other feeling, and in time you'll see that it's just a passing mind state like any other. This understanding will give you more confidence in your practice.

You will of course encounter other challenges when meditating, and you'll need to bring your knowing awareness to acknowledge whatever's there. We want to invite you to expand your perception and be open to something new.

Establishing an Informal Practice of Mindfulness: Mindfulness in Daily Activities

As previously mentioned, mindfulness is a way of life that can be practiced both formally and informally. We want to invite you to begin incorporating mindfulness into your daily activities as a way of decreasing panic.

Bringing mindfulness into your life is very important in dealing with panic. As with formally practicing mindfulness, you can do this every day. Daily mindfulness brings awareness into your body, emotions, and thoughts in the varied experiences of everyday living. You can bring mindfulness to chores, work, walking, driving, brushing your teeth, folding laundry, waiting in line, sitting in the doctor's office, your interpersonal relationships, and all aspects of life. The only moment you ever really live in and the only place you can ever make any changes is right here and now, so why not be mindful of this moment?

To begin an informal practice of mindfulness, you can start with any of the suggestions below. The more you do them, the more they'll become integrated into your life. Accomplish at least one task each day mindfully. In other words, while you're doing something, just be doing that one thing, fully present and attentive to what you're doing. There's no need to be a perfectionist here—it won't be possible to be mindful of all of these activities all the time—but slowly you can do more activities mindfully. Remember, the moment you realize you aren't present, you are. It's that close and yet that far. Let there be a spirit of levity, kindness, and self-compassion with this practice of mindfulness—this is why it's called a practice. Don't feel as if you have to "get it right" every time.

* When you wake up, take a mindful breath and then notice and acknowledge how you're feeling in your body and mind.

* While getting dressed, be mindful of the clothes you're selecting for the day. Notice how they feel when you put them on.

* While brushing your teeth, just be brushing your teeth.

* While preparing and eating breakfast, be mindful of the preparation and how the food tastes.

* While washing the dishes, just be washing the dishes.

* While folding the laundry, be mindful of the folding and how it's feeling.

* While walking, just be walking. Notice each step.

* While driving to work, drive the speed limit, turn off the radio, and be aware of driving your car. Notice the way your body feels while driving,

* At work, be mindful of your work duties and your inter-actions with others.

* At least once a week, eat a meal in silence, without distractions— radio, TV, newspaper, and so on—using the time to just experience eating.

* Choose a commonplace sight, sound, or occurrence— such as a red light, waiting in line, the phone ringing, or the sound of office machines warming up—as a cue for you to re-center and come back to yourself for a few mindful breaths (see "Foundational Practice: Mindful Breathing" in chapter 1).

* Be mindful of errands and interactions you have with others while you're out.

* Be mindful while you're on the phone, using e-mail, or text messaging.

* Be mindful of how you communicate with your family, friends, acquaintances, and even strangers.

* Be mindful of your evening activities, such as eating, reading, watching TV, and interacting with your family.

* As you head to bed, be mindful of your various bedtime activities: brushing your teeth, changing your clothes, and climbing into bed and lying down.

* Before you go to sleep, check in with how you're feeling physically, mentally, and emotionally, and let it all be. Take a few mindful breaths and let yourself open to deeper compassion and ease of your body and mind, and go into a deep, restful sleep.

These are just a few ways you can informally practice mindfulness. Feel free to bring more and more mindfulness into whatever you do. Remember: wherever you go, here you are. A practice of bringing your awareness into the here and now will help you stay centered and reduce moments of panic.

chapter 1

Calming the Rush of Panic in Your Body

Your body, emotions, and thoughts all play a role in panic. Learning how to work with them can help you stay centered and calm. In this chapter we look at ways that you can reduce the panic in your body. We will introduce you to two mindfulness meditations that focus on the body. The first is mindful breathing, and the second is the body scan. For each meditation, we provide a script you can follow, as well as a URL so you can download an audio track to guide you. Then we discuss the mindful practice called S.T.O.P. Finally we offer some practical applications of mindfulness for you to try, to help you feel more confident and comfortable in your own skin.

So that you feel safe, before you begin we'd like to offer some gentle suggestions regarding all of the meditations and other practices in this book: Please tread lightly. The meditations, informal practices, and applied practices are meant not to create more panic or pressure in your life but as a way to help you practice engaging with panic in safe and relatively com-fortable surroundings. Know that you can stop at any time. Please take care of yourself in the best way you need to. Remember: easy does it; one step at a time. Slowly and gradually you can learn to live with more ease.

Mindful Breathing

Mindful breathing is part of the foundation of MBSR and often our first recommendation to anyone living with the challenges of panic. It involves diaphragmatic or abdominal breathing, also known as belly breathing, which is very helpful in calming the body because it's the way that you naturally breathe when asleep or relaxed.

Take a moment right now to be mindful of your breath. Gently place your hands on your belly. Breathe normally and naturally. When you breathe in, simply be aware that you're breathing in; when you breathe out, be aware that you're breathing out. Feel your belly rise and fall with your breath. Now take two more mindful breaths and then continue reading.

The reason diaphragmatic or abdominal breathing is con-sidered an "anti-panic/anxiety" breath is that it helps regulate irregular breathing patterns fairly quickly. Often when you feel panicked, your breathing will become rapid, irregular, and shallow. You'll tend to breathe mostly in your chest and neck. When you shift to diaphragmatic breathing, this will help regu-late the breath so you can begin to feel more balanced and relaxed.

FOUNDATIONAL PRACTICE:
Mindful Breathing

Find a quiet place where you can be undisturbed. Turn off your phone and any other devices that might take you away from this special time that you're giving yourself. Assume a posture in which you can be comfortable and alert, whether sitting in a chair or on a cushion or lying down.

You can learn mindful breathing by reading the script below, pausing briefly after each paragraph. Aim for a total time of at least five minutes. You're welcome to download a (fifteen-minute) recording from New Harbinger Publications at newharbinger.com/25264.

Take a few moments to congratulate yourself that you are taking some time for meditation.

Now bring awareness to the breath in the abdomen or belly, breathing normally and naturally. As you breathe in, be aware of breathing in; as you breathe out, be aware of breathing out. If it is helpful, place your hands on your belly to feel it expand with each inhalation and contract with each exhalation. Simply maintaining this awareness of the breath, breathing in and breathing out. If you are unable to feel the breath in your belly, find some other way— place your hands on your chest, or feel the movement of air in and out of your nostrils.

There's no need to visualize, count, or figure out the breath. Just being mindful of breathing in and out. Without judgment, just watching, feeling, experiencing the breath as it ebbs and flows. There's no place to go and nothing else to do. Just being in the here and now, mindful of your breathing, living life one inhalation and one exhalation at a time.

As you breathe in, feel the abdomen or belly expand or rise like a balloon inflating, then feel it receding or deflating or falling on the exhalation. Just riding the waves of the breath, moment by moment, breathing in and out.

From time to time, you may notice that your attention has wandered from the breath. When you notice this, just acknowledge that your mind wandered and acknowledge where it went, and then bring your attention gently back to the breath.

Remember, there is no other place to go, nothing else you need to do, and no one you have to be right now. Just breathing in and breathing out.

Breathing normally and naturally, without manipulating the breath in any way, just being aware of the breath as it comes and goes.

As you come to the end of this meditation, congratulate yourself that you took this time to be present and that you are directly cultivating inner resources for healing and well-being. Let us take a moment to end this meditation with the wish "May all beings be at peace."

*

How to Practice Mindful Breathing

Give yourself the gift of formally practicing this meditation every day, even for a short period. It might be helpful to start off practicing mindful breathing for five minutes once a day and build it up from there. Maybe you'll find that you can add a second or even a third five-minute session, practicing mindful breathing at different times of your day. You can get additional benefit if you gradually extend your mindful breathing to ten, fifteen, twenty, or even thirty minutes at least once a day. Let this be a part of your practice of mindfulness that you look forward to doing, a special time for you to center yourself and "return home" to your being. Feel free to use an alarm clock or timer; you can download free meditation timers from the Insight Meditation Center (http://www.insightmeditationcenter.org /meditation-timers/) that feature a pleasant sound.

Like other meditations offered in this book, mindful breathing can be incorporated into your daily activities too. As far as where to practice informally, just about anywhere works. Take a few minutes at home, at work, at the doctor's office, at the bus stop, or even while waiting in line to bring a little mindful breathing into your life. You can also make it a habit to take a few mindful breaths right after you wake up, when you take a morning break, at lunchtime, in the afternoon, at night, or right before you go to sleep. Once you've practiced mindful breathing at these times, you can experiment with using it when you're feeling some angst, to help you calm the rush of panic in your body.

❋ Jane's Story

Jane had lived with panic for a long time, and it prevented her from fully living her life. Even going to the store stirred up feelings of panic for Jane. She wished that she had more self-confidence so that she could take on bigger challenges, but she didn't know what to do. Sometimes she wondered whether she would ever be successful.

One day, Jane heard from a friend she hadn't seen in a while, Tom, who also lived with panic. Tom told her about a breathing practice that he'd learned at an MBSR class. He said that it was helping him a lot. Jane was skeptical at first. *Breathing? Ha!* she thought. *I breathe all the time, and it doesn't help me!* However, the next time she saw Tom—who had formerly been so wracked with panic he could barely go out at all— she was staggered to see him not only functioning but living much better. He even seemed happy. Tom showed Jane how to do breathe mindfully, and she began practicing it.

Jane felt that deliberately taking the time to practice mindful breathing helped her calm down, and this gave her a very practical and useful tool she could bring into her life wherever she went. Even as she walked to the post office down the street, Jane could practice her breathing to stay centered. As she began to feel at ease within herself, she grew in confidence that she had the inner resources to deal with her panic, and she knew that she was on the right track. Gradually she began to feel better and regain some of the life that she felt as if she had lost. Her self-confidence soared, and she began to explore the world around her with greater curiosity and enjoyment.

The Body Scan

The body scan is another meditation that can help you deal with panic, anxiety, or fear by first sensing or feeling into the body with mindfulness. By practicing the body scan you'll learn to bring your attention directly into your body, part by part, to feel and acknowledge whatever's present—physically, emotionally, and mentally.

As you scan your body you may discover physical tension or pain, as well as strong emotions of panic, sadness, or anger. The practice is to be mindful and nonjudgmental and to acknowledge whatever you're feeling. If you have sensations of tightness, see whether you can allow them to soften, and if you're unable to do so, then let them be—let the waves of sensations ripple or resonate wherever they need to go. Just as the sky gives room for a storm, make space for what you're feeling physically or mentally. By acknowledging your body, emotions, and thoughts rather than suppressing, denying, or repressing them, you'll become less burdened by them.

You can learn the body scan by reading the script below, pausing after each paragraph for a short time to focus on the parts you've been instructed to meditate upon, or you're welcome to download a fifteen-, thirty-, or forty-five-minute recording from New Harbinger Publications at newharbinger.com/25264.

FOUNDATIONAL PRACTICE:
The Body Scan

Get yourself settled into a quiet place where you can be left undisturbed. Turn off your phone or any other device that might take you away from this special time that you're giving yourself. Find a posture in which you can be comfortable and alert. You're welcome to sit on a chair or cushion, or you can lie down on your bed or the carpet.

(Note: Some people find the body scan very relaxing and like to use it at bedtime as a way to fall asleep, as we describe later in this chapter. This is fine, especially if you have difficulties falling or staying asleep. If it's not bedtime, however, try to stay awake during the body scan, to get other important benefits from it. If you find yourself unintentionally falling asleep, make an adjustment—if you're lying down, for example, try sitting up.)

First, take a moment to congratulate yourself for taking this time for meditation.

Begin by checking in with yourself to see how you are feeling physically, mentally, and emotionally, and just let it be. There's no need to judge, analyze, or figure things out. Just allowing yourself to be in the here and now, just as you are.

Now gently shift your focus to the breath, becoming aware of your breath moving in and out of your nostrils or causing your belly to rise and fall. Breathing in and knowing breathing in; breathing out and knowing breathing out.

There will be times that your mind will wander from the breath, and when you recognize this, just acknowledge it and then come back to the breath, breathing in and out.

And now gently withdraw your attention from mindful breathing, and before we move into the body scan we would like to offer you an introduction to it. As you prepare to go through your body part by part, be mindful of what you are experiencing at first physically and sensationally. There may be times that the feelings in your body evoke emotions and thoughts—if that happens, just let that be part of your meditation, to be acknowledged as part of your practice. If you feel any anxiety or panic, just acknowledge it and let it be, allowing yourself to ride the waves of its sensations, just giving it space to run its course.

Also in regard to the body, perhaps you have had some parts surgically removed or replaced. You may have added parts such as surgical screws, plates, and most commonly dental fillings. Maybe you are living with an illness or pain that has affected your body in a number of ways. Whatever shape or situation you find your body in, please be mindful and acknowledge whatever is evoked physically, mentally, or emotionally, and let it be.

Now let's begin the body scan by bringing your attention to the bottom of the left foot, sensing into where you feel your foot making contact with the floor or another surface.

Gradually expand your awareness to the entire bottom of the left foot, then to the toes, then to the top of the foot, then into the heel and the lower Achilles tendon area, and then up to the left ankle, sensing whatever is present.

Now expand to the lower left leg, feeling into the calf and shin and its connection to the knee. Being present.

Remind yourself from time to time to be mindful of whatever thoughts or emotions you have as a result of feeling the sensations in your body.

Letting awareness now rise up into the thigh, sensing into the upper leg and its connection to the left hip.

And now, withdrawing your awareness from the left hip down to the left foot and shifting it into the right foot, again beginning at that point where you feel your foot making contact with the floor or another surface.

Then gradually expanding your awareness to the entire bottom of the right foot, then to the toes, then to the top of the foot, then into the heel and the lower Achilles tendon area, and then up to the right ankle, sensing and feeling into your right foot and ankle.

Now expanding your attention to the lower right leg, feeling into the calf and shin and its connection to the knee, being present.

Letting your awareness now rise up into the thigh. Sensing into the upper leg and its connection to the right hip.

Gently withdrawing your attention from the right hip and moving it into the pelvic region. Sensing into the systems of elimination and reproduction. Being present.

Remembering to be mindful from time to time of whatever the sensations in your body evoke emotionally and mentally. If you come across feelings of panic, acknowledge them and let them be, allowing yourself to ride the waves of panic, just giving it space to run its course.

Now gently shifting your focus from the pelvic region to the abdomen and into the belly—the great home of digestion and assimilation—feeling into your guts with awareness and letting be.

And now bringing your awareness into the tailbone and sensing into the lower, middle, and upper parts of the back, noticing sensations, allowing any tightness to soften if possible and, if not possible, then letting those sensations be. Let the sensations ripple in whatever direction they need to take. Being present.

Letting your awareness now travel around to the front of the body: into the skin of the chest, then through the breasts, then gently inward into the rib cage and sternum, and then into the lungs and the heart, being present.

Remembering from time to time to be mindful and acknowledging any thoughts and emotions, including panic, sadness, or anger, riding their waves and letting be.

Withdrawing your attention from the chest and shifting your awareness to the tips of the fingers of the left hand. Feeling into the fingers, then into the palm, and then to the top of the hand and up into the left wrist.

Proceeding up into the forearm, then elbow, then upper left arm, and then left shoulder, noticing sensations.

And now shifting your awareness to the tips of the fingers of the right hand. Feeling into the fingers, then the palm, then the top of the hand, and then the right wrist.

Proceeding up into the forearm, then elbow, then upper right arm, and then shoulder. Being present—feeling into the right arm with your awareness.

Letting your awareness now expand fully into both shoulders and armpits and then up into the neck and throat, being present, remembering from time to time to be mindful and acknowledging any thoughts and emotions, including panic, sadness, or anger, riding their waves and letting be.

And now bringing your awareness into the hinge of the jaw and then gently into the teeth, then the tongue, and then the lips, allowing any resonating rings of sensations to go wherever they need to go and letting be.

Feeling into the chin and up to the cheeks, then to the sinus passages that go deep inside the head, then to the eyes and the muscles around the eyes. Feeling into the forehead and the temples, being present.

Expanding your awareness now into the top and back of the head, then into the ears, and then into the inside of the head to the brain, being present and acknowledging anything you are feeling physically, mentally, or emotionally and letting be.

Now expanding the field of your awareness to the entire body, from head to toes to fingertips, connecting the head to the neck, to the shoulders, arms, hands, chest, back, belly, hips, pelvic region, legs, and feet.

Feeling the body as a whole organism, being present.

Breathing in, feeling the whole body rising and expanding, and breathing out, feeling it falling and contracting, being mindful of whatever is arising physically, mentally, or emotionally and letting be—being present.

As you come to the end of the body scan, take a moment first to open your eyes, wiggle your fingers and toes, and just be here and now. In a few minutes you will get up and go on with your day. Congratulate yourself for taking this time to be present and for directly participating in your health and well-being.

"May all beings be at peace."

*

How to Practice the Body Scan

The body scan is an important meditation to help you get in touch with your body and mind. This is great training for dealing with panic and to gradually begin to feel more acceptance and ease within yourself.

As you practice the body scan, there may be at times a feeling that it's counterintuitive at first to acknowledge what you're feeling physically, mentally, and emotionally. In time, you'll gradually come to know the skillfulness and efficiency of this. You'll recognize that acknowledging your feelings becomes a powerful mechanism of emotional discharge and release. You'll begin to gain confidence that the best way to straighten out is to turn in the direction of the skid. Perhaps you've noticed that the more you try to avoid your feelings, the more they return—again and again—just as when you turn away from a skid, the car spins out of control. The body scan teaches you to mindfully go with what's happening rather than fighting it. See what happens when you do this in your own life.

By doing the body scan once (or maybe even twice) a day, you'll learn how to work with a whole range of sensations, thoughts, and feelings. Try to make time to do the body scan when you can; even a short period will benefit you as you get in touch with your body. Feel free to use an alarm clock or timer, but always try to find a quiet place where you can be uninterrupted for the duration of your practice. Some people like to do the body scan in the morning before getting out of bed, while others prefer mid-morning, the lunch hour, or before or after dinner. Some prefer to practice right before going to bed. There is no right time other than the time you pick to do it.

Let this be a part of your practice of mindfulness you look forward to doing, a gift to yourself and a way to become more balanced within your being.

✳ *Marcos's Story*

Marcos had a regular job, but he dreaded leaving the house to go to work. His frequent panic attacks drained his confidence and trust in himself and left him feeling defeated.

Sometimes the panic attacks he experienced nearly every day seemed to make sense, like when he was driving in traffic, giving a speech, or talking at a meeting, but some attacks didn't make any sense at all. They seemed to come for no apparent reason, just out of the blue. Sometimes just the thought of being in a difficult situation would make his heart pound, make his palms sweat, and leave him practically gasping for air. A doctor checked him out to see whether there was any physical condition underlying his panic, but the workup revealed nothing remarkable. The doctor told Marcos that he needed to learn how to live his life with less panic.

Marcos talked with his wife, Juanita, about this. Juanita did some research and found out about MBSR and that it had been shown to be helpful in treating panic. She told Marcos that MBSR was evidence-based, meaning scientifically proven. Marcos realized that he had to do something and decided to give it a shot. He felt as though he had nothing to lose.

In his first MBSR class, when the other attendees began to introduce themselves and share why they were there, cold sweat started to pour from Marcos's palms. He wasn't sure that he'd be able to talk, and when it was the person next to him's turn to speak, Marcos felt as though he was going to implode or blow up. The teacher thankfully noticed this and asked the class to pause for a moment. The teacher looked directly at Marcos with caring eyes, and with much compassion she announced that if anyone wanted to pass, that would be fine, because what was most important was to have a safe environment. Marcos inwardly sighed with relief. He felt kindness, he felt seen, and he felt honored. After the person next to him spoke, Marcos felt enough trust to muster and open his mouth and heart and share how panic had taken over his life. These were incredible first steps for Marcos, and he was surprised to discover that he wasn't the only one in the class who lived with panic—there were actually a few others. At the end of the class, a few people even came over to Marcos to congratulate him for having the courage to speak. Marcos drove home that evening filled with hope and encouragement, for the first time he could remember.

Marcos began practicing the body scan and took to it like a fish to water. He practiced every day and sometimes twice or even three times a day. Marcos began to reconnect with his body and mind. He began to feel more trust in himself. He learned to acknowledge all his feelings in his body and mind. He felt like a new man, and it seemed to him that many possibilities were opening up in his life. He began to feel comfortable inside his own skin as he allowed himself to feel the totality of his being, his life.

S.T.O.P.

A wonderful practice from MBSR that we'd like you to use in your informal practice of mindfulness is called S.T.O.P. In this exercise, you simply put whatever you're doing on hold for a quick breather and to realize what's going on with you. This helps restore your balance, like pushing your "reset" button, so you can proceed feeling renewed and refreshed. The acronym S.T.O.P. helps you remember the following steps:

* Stop.

* Take a breath.

* Observe, acknowledge, and allow what's here.

* Proceed and be present.

It's truly amazing what you can learn about yourself when you pause from time to time to breathe, observe, acknowledge, and allow how you're feeling physically, mentally, and emotionally. A colleague of ours who programmed her computer to display the word "S.T.O.P." once an hour as a reminder often mentioned how amazed she was, upon stopping, to discover that her shoulders were higher than her ears or that she'd just been spinning around in circles in her mind and hardly getting any work done because she really needed to use the restroom. At other times she discovered that she was hungry or needed to stretch or go on a break. When she realized what she needed and took care of her body or mind, her work became easier and she was more efficient, relaxed, and happy. This simple and yet profound exercise will help you connect more with your life. It's a proactive approach to panic or stress that will make you feel generally more stable and in control.

You can also do this practice when you feel panicked. When a moment of panic arises, take a breath; this will help you bring your breath back into your belly. Then observe, acknowledge, and allow whatever you're feeling in your body and mind. This will help you settle down and realize that you do have some control or a way to deal with this. Lastly, proceed with your day and be present. You can of course repeat this sequence a few times to help you relax further.

In her poem "Allow," Danna Faulds (2002) shares her wisdom on how to transform life's challenges by learning to go with the flow of life.

> There is no controlling life.
> Try corralling a lightning bolt,
> containing a tornado. Dam a
> stream and it will create a new
> channel. Resist, and the tide
> will sweep you off your feet.
> Allow, and grace will carry
> you to higher ground. The only
> safety lies in letting it all in—
> the wild and the weak; fear,
> fantasies, failures and success.
> When loss rips off the doors of
> the heart, or sadness veils your
> vision with despair, practice
> becomes simply bearing the truth.
> In the choice to let go of your
> known way of being, the whole
> world is revealed to your new eyes.

When you take time to practice mindful breathing, the body scan, and S.T.O.P., you naturally begin to utilize the mindfulness attitudes (discussed in the Foundation chapter) of intention, beginner's mind, nonjudgment, nonstriving, allowing, letting be, self-reliance, balance, and self-compassion. These are important allies for your practice and well-being.

You can then apply what you're learning to your everyday life to help you deal with the rush of panic in your body.

Applied Practices

Following we describe several applications of mindfulness that you can use in your informal practice of mindfulness. Please don't worry about the "right" or "wrong" way to do these; by just giving them a try, you're on your way to a more mindful and panic-free life.

KICK OFF A GOOD DAY

If your morning starts off with the news, like mine does, a barrage of negative headlines can inch your body toward panic without your even being aware of it. The weather reports a storm heading your way, someone was murdered, and somewhere a war has broken out. Chronic bad news can have profound effects on your body—your neck and shoulders tighten, your stomach churns, and your whole being goes on heightened alert. You don't have to give up your daily dose of morning news, but we recommend that you start each morning with the following version of the S.T.O.P. practice, in order that you might have more balance and ease in your body as your day begins.

1. Upon waking, with your eyes open, take this moment to stop and pause. You can be lying in your bed, sitting up, or standing. In the pause, just let your body relax and be still. Give yourself permission to just be here, floating adrift for a minute or two, before you rush into your hectic day of endless to-dos.

2. If you're experiencing panic at this time, take a breath. Tune in to your breathing. If you're holding your breath, take this time to gradually let the air flow freely in and out of your belly. Notice the air in your nose, in your chest, and in your abdomen. When your mind starts to drift, return to your breath again, and be mindful of each inhalation and exhalation—the rhythm, flow, sound, and sensation in your body.

3. Observe your body and whatever feelings or sensations are stirring in it. Where are you feeling tension or tightness? Where are you feeling relaxed and at ease? Where are you feeling panic? Take this time to acknowledge what you notice. Whatever your body is feeling—tension, stiffness, dry mouth, shortness of breath—let it just be. Pay attention to your body's experience.

4. Discover what you may need right now to take better care of your body and connect more fully with your life. You may need a drink of water. You may need a morning of music or silence instead of grim news. You may need a longer shower than usual. Think of how you can gain a sense of inner balance and anchor yourself in this balance throughout the rest of your day.

5. Proceed with your morning and be present. Remember to reflect on what came up for you during this application of mindfulness and what you learned about your body.

Feel free to repeat daily or at any time to help you maintain balance and ease in your body.

*

START YOUR MORNING
WITH MINDFULNESS

Mornings can be a time of rush and panic. The anticipation of the entire day buried under an avalanche of commitments and responsibilities stretched out in front of you may be daunting, even terrifying. You may experience an acute feeling of impending doom. You may feel paralyzed by fear, literally unable to move or get out of bed. Your heart may pound. You may have a sensation of choking or being smothered and start to hyperventilate. And yet, you somehow do eventually struggle out of bed and reluctantly start your day.

Most people's morning routine is fraught with potentially mindless tasks, such as brushing their teeth. When you wake up with feelings of impending doom, make up your mind to brush your teeth with mindfulness. Mindfulness will help you move more gently through your morning panic and restore a sense of calm and order in your body for the rest of your day.

1. Before you pick up your toothbrush, take a few deep breaths. Take several full breaths, tuning in to the cool air passing through your nose on the inhale and the warm air passing through your mouth or nose on the exhale. Be mindful of each breath and notice how it feels in your body.

2. Set your intentions aloud or to yourself for brushing your teeth mindfully. State what you would like to gain by this practice. You may say: *May this practice bring me more closely connected to my body. May this practice restore balance to my*

mind and body. Feel free to fill in your own words of what you'd like to experience as a result of your application of mindfulness.

3. As you begin your tooth-brushing routine, move slowly, methodically, and consciously. Pick up your toothbrush and notice all the tiny bristles. Notice the weight of the tooth-brush and how it feels in your hand. As you hold your toothbrush under the running water, notice whether you prefer warm or cold water. Notice whether you leave the water running or shut it off when you're done. As you apply the toothpaste, notice something about it too. Is it mint or some other flavor? Does it have a scent? How much tooth-paste is left in the tube?

4. Remember to return to the present moment by returning to your breath.

5. If you notice some doubt emerge, or a little voice saying *This exercise won't work. It can't help me with my panic,* simply acknowledge and observe these feelings of doubt, without making any judgments about them. Doubt is a normal mind state that occasionally springs up and tries to steer you away from the present moment. This is simply how you feel in this moment, and each moment is passing, just as everything in life is continually changing.

6. Begin to brush your teeth, paying attention to how you maneuver the brush and what sensations you feel in your mouth. Do you brush in small, circular motions or just back

and forth across your teeth? Notice the feeling of the tooth-paste foaming. Remember to stay present and connected to your breathing.

7. When you're ready to rinse your mouth, turn your aware-ness to the water and how it feels swirling and swishing in your mouth.

8. After you've rinsed, guide your tongue along your teeth and acknowledge the smoothness and freshness that you feel.

9. Take a brief moment to reflect on what's going on with your mind and body right now. Are you still holding a sensation of dread and of impending doom, or has it started to subside? Let whatever you're feeling just be what it is. Acknowledge the transient nature of these sensations, and let them come and go of their own accord.

10. Take a few more breaths before returning to your morning duties.

We used tooth brushing as an example, but you can apply a mindful approach to any routine morning task. Each habitual action is an opportunity to be more mindful and more engaged with your physical body. When you practice mindfulness during these tedious but necessary tasks, you deepen your awareness of the present moment, the only moment in which you're truly alive and can make changes in your life.

*

WASH AWAY YOUR PANIC

Have you ever had a panic attack in your sleep? One woman told us that on many mornings she'd wake up trembling in a cold sweat. On these occasions she ached for a long, hot bath before starting her day, but she never had the time.

Few people have time for a long soak in the bath before work. A brisk shower is the best most of us can hope for to wash away sleep and pull ourselves together for the long day ahead. And sadly, showers can also be another part of a mindless routine, a task that we do simply to get it over with and get on with our day. Everyday activities are perfect opportunities for cultivating mindfulness. Perhaps you might consider each shower as a cleansing ritual, approaching it as a symbolic act of washing away the panicky sensations trapped in your mind and body. In this next practice you'll do just that, step by step, breath by breath.

1. Before you run the water or get in the shower, take a few breaths. Each breath links you closer to the present moment, right here and now.

2. Set your intentions for this mindful practice. You may say aloud or to yourself: *May this shower bring me into my body. May this shower help me be with things as they are and ease my body and mind.*

3. Once the water temperature is set to your liking, step carefully and slowly into the shower. Experience this moment with all your senses—touch, taste, sound, smell, and sight.

What does the water feel like on your face, arms, chest, back, and legs? What sounds are coming from the water? What fragrances do you notice from your soap, shampoo, or shaving cream? Notice the steam collecting on the curtain, mirror, or glass surfaces.

4. Remember to tune in to your breathing while you continue to shower.

5. On your next inhale, recognize any feelings that your body is trying to relay to you. You may experience fear tightening your throat, making it hard to swallow. If so, allow the water to wash over your neck and be conscious of your intentions from step 2. You may experience anxiety making your lower back tense. If so, take this moment to let the warm water wash over and loosen those aching muscles as you breathe out.

6. For the rest of your shower, continue to pay attention to your body in this mindful and attentive manner, listening in on what your body needs. By doing so, you're fostering a new kind of relationship with your body and your body's experience of panic.

Let morning showers be your special time for you to mindfully check in with yourself, each warm droplet of water replenishing and healing to your mind and body.

*

DRIVE WITH MORE EASE

A panic attack can occur at any time and without warning. You may panic at inopportune times, such as while driving: going into a tunnel, crossing a bridge, or heading into a busy intersection. If this often happens to you, when you feel your heart pound in your throat and you start to clutch the steering wheel tightly, it's okay to pull over for a bit. Find the nearest freeway exit or otherwise safely get off the road or highway. Then, take a break for a little mindful breathing. Practicing mindful breathing at such times will come in handy, even for the times that you struggle with panic when you can't safely exit or park your car someplace. At those times, simply bringing to mind the memory of an episode in which you used mindful breathing may help. The instructions below are for you to practice ahead of time, while you're not operating a vehicle.

1. Find a quiet place to sit or stand in silence. Turn off your cell phone, computer, TV, or any other distractions. Acknowledge to yourself that this is your quality time for self-reflection. Be alert and pay attention to your posture, finding a comfortable position for your body to support itself. You can keep your eyes open or close them, but remain alert and focused.

2. Take this time to focus on your breathing. Notice what's happening with your breath. Are you short of breath or breathing steadily? Are you breathing from your mouth or nose, your chest or your belly? The chest is where you typically breathe when you're panicked or feeling anxious. As you begin to pay more attention to your breath, try placing

one hand on your chest, one hand on your belly, and then practice returning your breath to your belly. The belly is where you'll find release from stress in the body. Follow each breath in and out, in and out again. Feel your lungs fill with air and empty of air, filling and emptying over and over again. Notice the rise and fall of your hand on your belly, rising and falling with each breath. Belly moves up on the inhale. Belly drops on the exhale.

3. When you notice that thoughts arise or something distracts your attention, acknowledge where you went and bring your mind back to your breathing. This is a good time to notice your responses, reactions, and sensations and then return to the present moment through your breath or perhaps by focusing on a single sound or object. You may hear the laughter of kids on the street, you may hear the rain on your roof, or you may notice a chill in the room or an old favorite sweater left out. Sometimes your mind will want to wander, and that's normal; simply notice what your mind is focusing on and then gently return your attention to your breath—in and out, rising and falling, on and on.

4. You may say aloud or to yourself: *With each breath, I am acknowledging any sensations that arise, without judgment. With each breath, I am observing how all sensations come and go. With each breath, I am learning to ride the waves of my panic and let be.*

Diaphragmatic breathing, as in mindful breathing, is a beneficial form of deep relaxation. We encourage you to practice breathing from your belly several times a day, until it becomes a

GIVE A WORRY-FREE PRESENTATION

If your job requires making speeches or giving presentations, your panic may shoot through the roof on a weekly basis no matter how many times you rehearse. You may feel on edge, startle easily, get butterflies in your stomach, feel jumpy and unsettled, or sweat profusely. Mindfulness can be a powerful antidote to the panicky feelings that may precede every speech or presentation. This next mindful practice will help anchor your mind and body in your breath in order to build concentration and focus before you have to perform in front of an audience. Go ahead and try it now.

1. First, settle into a comfortable and quiet space and sitting position. Be aware of your posture, sitting tall and alert.

2. Think of your panicky sensations as being somewhere on a dial. At one end of the dial, the panicky energy is expansive and high volume. At the other end, the panicky energy is diminished and low volume.

3. Take several thoughtful, slow breaths and then just pay attention to your breathing. Your lungs naturally expand and contract, filling and releasing with air, of their own accord. As you proceed, return to the breath as often as you can, which will help your mind focus and be present.

4. In terms of your experience of panic in this moment, you may be at various points on the dial at different times. Check in with yourself on where your sensations of panic

are showing up on your dial. Where do you fall on a 0 to 10 scale, if 10 is the highest volume and 0 is the lowest volume? Are you at a 3 or a 5 or an 8?

5. Once you've selected the number that best represents your degree of panic in this moment, on your next inhale, say aloud or to yourself: *I am acknowledging any sensations that arise in my body.* Exhale: *I am aware that each sensation is neither good nor bad; it simply is.* Inhale: *I am observing and experiencing the coming and going of each sensation and letting it be.* Exhale: *I am noticing how sensations are not permanent states of being, but always passing and changing.* Try this for four to eight breaths.

6. One of the challenges that you may experience before you perform in front of an audience is restlessness. Your body may grow agitated, unable to relax and be still. This is your mind's way of distracting you, preventing you from being fully engaged in the present moment. If you're feeling stirred up and restless, simply acknowledge this sensation and observe it. There's no need to suppress or change it. Once you acknowledge it, you take away its power over you and you gradually return to being present again.

7. Take this moment to fully inhabit your body in the silence around you. Take this time to acknowledge your mind and body that writes and prepares speeches and presentations. When you're ready, move ahead with your presentation with enhanced concentration and focus.

*

GET GROUNDED

Panic has a way of throwing off your sense of connection and feelings of groundedness. People often express feeling disconnected, numb, or unsteady during times of panic. When you feel ungrounded because of panic, you might benefit from a walking meditation.

Before or after a meal is an ideal time for this mindful practice. Walking is an excellent way to get you feeling grounded and help you tune in to your body and mind. Gentle movement, such as walking, is soothing and helps quiet the mind. With regular practice, it can become a simple and supportive routine in your life. If you can walk barefoot, that's ideal, but it's okay with shoes as well. You can walk indoors or outdoors. What distance you walk isn't really important. You can walk down a hallway and back, for example, or you can walk around the block.

1. Set your intentions for your walk. Say aloud or to yourself: *I am walking to feel grounded and balanced. I am walking to make time for listening to and expanding my awareness of my body.*

2. Stand still and tall and strong, but also stand comfortably and at ease in your body. Your arms should be loose at your sides and your face forward. Your feet should be hip-distance apart. Tenderly shake out your shoulders to release any tension in them, and then take a few deep breaths.

3. Pay close attention to your feet on the ground. Notice the pressure under the soles of your feet. Gently shift your weight from left to right, and take a moment to feel your weight in your body. Your body may sway forward or backward, or side to side. Notice how this feels. Start to steady

yourself until you're still and find your center again. This center is where you're strongest and most grounded, like a firmly rooted tree.

4. Begin to take your first few steps, moving into a slow walk. Acknowledge how your feet feel with each step. What sensations are you experiencing in your toes? In your heels?

5. Become aware of what walking feels like in other parts of your body. What's happening in your ankles and calves? Your hips and torso? Your neck and arms?

6. Pay attention to your stride, your pace, and the rhythm of your walking.

7. If your mind starts to get distracted by various thoughts and worries, gently bring your attention back to your body and what feelings are arising during your walk.

8. When you're ready to complete your walk, return to a standing position as before. Feel the stillness in your body. Take a deep breath and send a warm blessing of gratitude to your feet.

When you take time to tune in to the physical sensations of your body—before, during, or after a panic attack—you deepen your appreciation for your body. You become more mindful of the needs of your body. Your body has a voice, and it craves attention and nurturing. Practicing mindful walking daily will keep you grounded and help you stay connected to your body so that you might listen to it better. Set an intention to walk mindfully to your car or to work or to the bus stop each day.

*

FIND BALANCE

There's nothing worse than having a panic attack in public, like during a meeting at work or when you're waiting in line at a market or gas station. Your panic may inflame your body like a raging inferno. Physically, you may feel dizzy or reel with fear and bewilderment. Some people have described a sensation of vertigo or disorientation in their body at these times. The impulse to run out and get as far away from people as possible during a panic attack is undeniably real. You may experience a strong urge to postpone a transaction and rush frantically back to your car or your work station or even a vacant bathroom stall. That's okay. Just remember, you have other choices, and this book will teach you new ways to cope with the impulse to escape.

The following version of the S.T.O.P. practice will help you reclaim your sense of balance and strength to follow through with the task at hand, whether you're surrounded by strangers or people you know. Again, S.T.O.P. stands for Stop, Take a breath, Observe, and Proceed and be present. Try it now.

1. Begin by taking a pause and giving yourself permission to stop what you're doing. This is your special time to listen in and nurture yourself.

2. Pay attention to your breath. You may notice that you're holding your breath or that your breathing is constrained. If so, just let yourself breathe, without forcing it or changing your breath. Gradually, your breath will return and you'll connect with it more readily. When your breathing begins to feel more natural, normal, and steady, bring your breath into your belly. You may become aware of how your belly expands and contracts, pushing out against your clothing

on the inhale and then deflating on the exhale. Take a few belly breaths.

3. Observe, acknowledge, and allow any and all sensations that are coming up right now in your body. Are you feeling the urge to race out or to stay put? Are you dizzy or light-headed? Are you feeling more connected with your body or less connected? Acknowledge the feelings that your body is sharing with you. By allowing these sensations to surface and run their natural course, you'll start to settle down and recognize that you have more control than you often think. When you recognize the sensations percolating in your body, you create space for change and a way to work through these sensations, breath by breath, moment to moment.

4. Remember to breathe and return to being fully present in the now.

5. Move gently forward in your day. ("Move gently" is a common phrase used in mindful practices from yoga to meditation. Panic can make a person move about mind-lessly and without kindness toward the body. Be tender; move your body with kindness and awareness.) Be compassionate toward yourself when panicky feelings arise. They'll come and go, rise and fall, similar to your breath, and to the clouds overhead, and to the ebb and flow of the ocean.

S.T.O.P. is your free "time-out" ticket—time for just you, time to observe what's going on inside, and time to breathe. Your mindful awareness of your breath and your body is exactly where you'll discover your balance and equilibrium so that you can face the rest of your day with calm and ease.

*

GET A GOOD NIGHT'S REST

Panic can affect your sleep. At the end of your day, you may feel like a bundle of tired thoughts, feelings, and sensations, tied up in knots in various parts of your body. You may have difficulty falling asleep even days after a panic attack has subsided. If so, you're not alone. Long after the panic has faded, your body still struggles to let go of tightness in your chest, jaw, or hands. Wherever you hold your bodily stress, the following version of the body scan will help you find some of the relief you need in order to feel more at ease and hopefully get a restful sleep. With regular practice, three to four times a week before bed, your mind and body will begin to look forward to it and you'll experience a more peaceful sleep.

1. Locate a quiet space. Turn off electronic devices such as your cell phone, computer, radio, or TV. Feel free to dim the lights, if you prefer, or to set an alarm for ten to fifteen minutes—be sure to set the volume of the alarm to low. Wear comfortable, loose-fitting clothes, if possible.

2. Feel free to sit or lie down. Be comfortable but also be alert, aware, and mindful of your experience.

3. Begin by breathing slowly and smoothly and naturally.

4. As you continue to breathe, pay attention to your legs. When you breathe in, scan up and down your toes, feet, calves, thighs, and hips. Wherever you feel tension, continue to slowly breathe in and out, allowing yourself to feel the waves of sensations and acknowledging what you're

feeling physically, mentally, and emotionally. Do this for three full breaths, and let it all be.

5. Bring your attention to your torso. With each in-breath, scan up and down your pelvis, belly, chest, and spine. Wherever you notice stress, slowly breathe in and out. Do this for three full breaths, wherever the muscles are holding on, and let it be, offering no resistance, allowing nature to run its course.

6. Remember to pay attention and observe what's happening with your body.

7. Move on to your arms. With your next breath in, notice any sensations in your fingers, palms, wrists, forearms, biceps, and shoulders. With your next breath out, breathe naturally in and out and let the sensations be, neither pushing them away nor holding onto them. Follow this pattern for three full breaths. With each breath, imagine that you're slipping into a more peaceful space in your body.

8. Finally, scan along your neck and head. Notice any sensations in your throat, face, mouth, nose, eyes, forehead, and scalp. On your in-breath, continue to examine every muscle for places holding stress or tightness. On your out-breath, let the sensations be, following their own course like waves in the sea.

9. Breathe and scan. Sense and be aware. Notice how connected everything is right now, as you are resting gently. Continue to breathe and connect with your body.

10. If you start to feel sleepy, that's good. It's okay to surrender to your need for sleep.

May you have a restful and deep sleep.

*

Here We Are

As we come to the end of this chapter, you've been introduced to two MBSR foundational mindfulness meditations to help you deal with panicky feelings in your body: mindful breathing and the body scan. You've also learned the mindful practice S.T.O.P. We recommend that you continue to work with these as well as try incorporating some of the applied practices into your informal practice of mindfulness as outlined in the Foundation chapter. This is a recipe for a daily maintenance program to help decrease panic and live with more ease in your life. In the next chapter we investigate how mindfulness works with the strong emotions that panic evokes.

chapter 2

Calming the Rush of Panic in Your Emotions and Feelings

Panic affects you not only physically, but also in your emotions and feelings. The body and mind are integrally connected, and often when one is affected, the other is too. Learning how to work with the powerful emotions and feelings that come up with panic—such as terror, a feeling of impending doom, anxiety, worry, fear, anger, sadness, or shame—can be enormously liberating to the panicked heart.

As human beings, we are all affected by emotions. Most of us love to feel good and hate to feel bad. We want to be liked and accepted and despise or fear being disliked or discounted. There's a beautiful saying that people will always remember how you made them feel. Human beings are feeling beings, and it may often appear that your emotions are affected first before your thoughts. You can walk into a room and get a feel of a person or situation before you start thinking and assessing the situation to determine whether you feel comfortable or not.

Within the body, the feelings of panic are very distinct and visceral; there may be rapid breathing, a pounding heartbeat, and many other pronounced physical sensations. Equally, panic affects the mind with a strong array of emotions, feelings, and thoughts. Panicky feelings can arise as quickly as a flash of lightning and send powerful waves of impending doom that render you feeling out of control and not knowing what to do. Sometimes those feelings are beyond reasoning, for it feels as though they come out of nowhere. Other times, there may be unacknowledged emotions, wounds, or traumas from your past that have yet to be worked through with meaning and healing. Whether the origin of your panic is known to you or not, panic affects your body *and* mind.

In this chapter we would like to introduce you to mindful inquiry meditation, for your formal practice of mindfulness, and R.A.I.N., for your informal practice of mindfulness. Both of these can help you deal with emotions and feelings of panic. Let's begin with mindful inquiry meditation.

Mindful Inquiry

Mindful inquiry meditation is a very useful way to work with panic-stricken emotions and feelings. It is a meditative process of inquiring into the nature of what may be fueling or driving your panic. This type of inquiry is a form of investigation; it is not a process of analyzing, trying to figure things out, or making you feel better through positive thinking. It's a deep exploration of your body and mind, with a willingness to be in the unknown and the curiosity to see what's actually there.

This type of practice takes some willingness and courage, but if you really want to know what's fueling your panic, an investigation may sound quite reasonable. After all, what do you have to lose? It seems the only thing you have to lose is your panic. As President Franklin D. Roosevelt said, "All we have to fear is fear itself."

As a way to prepare you for this meditation, we would like to introduce you to two important aspects of mindful inquiry for working with panic. The first aspect is acknowledgment, and the second is letting be. You will discover that each supports the other in this process of investigation.

Acknowledgment and Letting Be

Acknowledgment is similar to one of the mindfulness attitudes: allowing. It is the practice of validating whatever's in your direct experience in a matter-of-fact way, just as a meteorologist reports the weather: it's 35 degrees, raining, and overcast; or it's 75, calm, and clear. In the same way, if you are feeling panicked, scared, or fearful, you directly acknowledge those feelings in your body and mind whether you're okay with them or not. Acknowledgment is this ability to see things just as they are without the filters of avoidance or grasping (disliking or liking).

Letting be was also discussed in the Foundation chapter as well as several places in chapter 1. It is another important aspect or quality that you can bring to acknowledgment. Letting be is different from letting go. Letting be is cultivating the ability to let things run their course rather than trying to push them away or adding on to them. How many times have you told yourself to let go of panic and it didn't work? If you could let go, you would have. Letting be is much more accessible, since you don't have to change anything. Letting be is learning to ride the waves of panic that are affecting you physically, mentally, or emotionally and allowing them to run their course, just like ripples from a rock thrown into a lake.

In the practice of mindful inquiry, please acknowledge whatever feelings of panic you may be experiencing in the body and mind and let them be. Learning how to go with the flow of life is a much more skillful approach to dealing with panic than fighting it. There's a wise saying: "Whatever you resist, persists." Although at first it may feel counterintuitive to turn toward your panic and acknowledge it and let it be, you may discover soon enough that as you learn to go with it rather than fighting it, it will begin to dissipate.

It's also important to note that when you begin to acknowledge feelings of panic, they may actually feel as though they are getting stronger. Please know this is a normal reaction. The reason it may feel like that is that you're actually bringing your light of awareness to the panic, rather than turning away from it. You will, however, discover that if you continue to ride its waves, acknowledging the feelings and letting them be, they will gradually subside. In time, you will grow in confidence, you will feel empowered, and the panic will not be able to consume or control you as much as before. You will learn that you don't have to be frightened and held hostage by your panic and fears and realize that you can live your life with greater ease and peace.

Deepening the Investigation

Mindful inquiry meditation is an investigation into what's fueling your panic, fear, or anxiety. The more you understand what's driving it, the more you can be free of it. When your awareness and understanding grows brighter, the darkness of panic and fear diminishes. So after acknowledging your panic and letting it be, you are welcome to proceed further into a deeper investigation into what's driving the panic. This is called mindful inquiry.

When you practice mindful inquiry, you may first want to try to calm your body and mind with some mindful breathing and then begin to acknowledge and let be whatever you're feeling physically, mentally, and emotionally. In this meditation you are going to stay and investigate those feelings of panic by bringing attention to the fearful feelings themselves. This is done by bringing awareness to the feeling of panic in your body and mind and letting yourself experience and investigate it non-judgmentally, just the way it is. Allow yourself to acknowledge what it feels like in your body, emotions, and feelings, and let these feelings be. There's no need to analyze or figure them out; just ride and observe and experience the waves of emotions and feelings as they come and go. In time you may discover that within those feelings of panic lie important insights into what may be fueling them. You may also realize that within you are tremendous resources for resiliency and healing—that you can learn to overcome those powerful and captive feelings of panic and live with more freedom and ease in your life.

Below is one poignant story of mindful inquiry. Although this story illustrates the recalling of childhood memories and trauma that fed into panic, we should mention that there are other kinds of insights and realizations you can gain from meditation, ones that may not have to do with repressed memories. Consider Marcos's story in the last chapter, in which his panic attacks seemed to come for no apparent reason. There are many reasons why people experience panic: past experiences, physiological or biological imbalances, diet, medicines, or drugs. Sometimes panic is truly enigmatic. What is of the utmost importance is how you respond and deal with it. That makes all the difference in the world.

✳ *Joe's Story*

For many years, one of my clients, Joe, had experienced panic when going over bridges. In session, I (Bob) suggested that we explore these feelings, and he agreed. I told him that he could stop at any point if it felt too uncomfortable. Joe began with mindful breathing, and then I gradually encouraged him to reflect on what it felt like to get near a bridge and to report any physical sensations, thoughts, or emotions that came up. He soon said that he was feeling tightness in his belly and chest and was beginning to feel scared. I instructed Joe to acknowledge those feelings, and in time he began to settle down. I invited him to move further into those feelings of tightness and to notice and acknowledge what it felt like physically and emotionally and to not analyze them. He was quiet for some time, and then he blurted out, "I remember! I remember when this all happened. I saw my sister get pushed off a bridge when I was a little boy." He went on to explain that it hadn't been a very large bridge—actually a culvert near where he grew up in a farm area—and that his sister fortunately had not been injured. Yet this was such a frightening experience for him that he had repressed this memory and developed a panic and anxiety disorder about going over bridges. This awareness helped free Joe from the panic.

In mindful inquiry you're invited to bring nonjudgmental awareness into any panicky emotions or feelings, whether they are related to memories (as in Joe's story) or not (as in Marcos's story), and to fully acknowledge and experience them in your body and mind and let them be. You may discover that within the panic is a whole plethora of feelings and experiences that are causing the agitation or whatever emotion you are feeling. When you begin to acknowledge what has not been acknowledged, the doorway of understanding can begin to open. By learning to turn toward your panic, you may experience more freedom than you could have ever imagined.

Before beginning this meditation, please consider whether this is the right time for you to do it. Do you feel reasonably safe and open? If not, do some mindful breathing and come back to it at another time.

FOUNDATIONAL PRACTICE:
Mindful Inquiry

In a quiet place, find a position in which you can be alert and comfortable, whether seated or lying down. Turn off your phone and any other electrical device that could disturb you. Read and practice the script for this guided meditation below, pausing after each paragraph, or feel free to download a thirty-minute version from New Harbinger Publications at newharbinger .com/25264.

First, congratulate yourself that you are dedicating some precious time to meditation.

Become aware of your body and mind and whatever you are carrying within you. Perhaps there are feelings from the day's events or whatever has been going on recently.

May you simply allow and acknowledge whatever is within you and let it be, without any form of analysis.

Gradually, shift the focus of awareness to the breath, breathing normally and naturally. As you breathe in, be aware of breathing in, and as you breathe out, be aware of breathing out.

Awareness can be focused at either the tip of the nose or the abdomen, depending on your preference. If focusing at the tip of the nose, feel the touch of the air as you breathe in and out… If focusing on the abdomen, feel the belly expanding on an inhalation and contracting on an exhalation.

Just living life, one inhalation and one exhalation at a time. Breathing in, breathing out, experiencing each breath appearing and disappearing. Just breathing.

And now gently withdraw awareness from the breath and shift to mindful inquiry.

Mindful inquiry is an investigation into emotions, thoughts, and physical sensations that are driving your panic, anxieties, and fears, often beneath the surface of your awareness. There is a special and unique way of doing this practice that can foster the potential for deep understanding and insight.

When you practice mindful inquiry, gently direct your attention into the bodily feeling of panic or fear itself. Allow yourself to bring nonjudgmental awareness into the experience of it, acknowledging whatever it feels like in the body and mind and letting it be.

To begin this exploration, you need to first check in with yourself and determine whether it feels safe. If you don't feel safe, perhaps it is better to wait and try another time and just stay with your breathing for now.

If you are feeling safe, then bring awareness into the body and mind and allow yourself to feel into and acknowledge any physical sensations, emotions, or thoughts, and just let them be...without trying to analyze or figure them out.

You may discover that within these feelings there's a multitude of thoughts, emotions, or old memories that are fueling your fears. When you begin to acknowledge what has not been acknowledged, the pathway of insight and understanding may arise. As you turn toward your emotions, they may show you what you are panicked, worried, mad, sad, or bewildered about.

You may learn that the very resistance to unacknowledged emotions often causes more panic or fear and that learning to go with it, rather than fighting it, often diminishes them. When we say "go with it," we mean that you allow and acknowledge whatever is within the mind and body. Just letting the waves of emotions, thoughts, and physical sensations go wherever they need to go, just like the sky makes room for any weather.

Now gently returning to the breath and being mindful of breathing in and out...riding the waves of the breath.

As you come to the end of this meditation, take a moment to congratulate yourself, and take a moment to appreciate the safety and ease you may be feeling right now that you can bring into your day. By acknowledging your fears, you may open the possibility for deeper understanding, compassion, and peace. Before you get up, gently wiggle your fingers and toes and gradually open your eyes, being fully here and now.

May all beings dwell in peace.

✱

How to Practice Mindful Inquiry

If you have connected with this meditation and find it useful, practice it whenever it feels right for you. This meditation is different from mindful breathing, the body scan, sitting meditation (chapter 3), and loving-kindness meditation (chapter 4), which you can work with daily. Those meditations are for building and maintaining balance and ease in your everyday life. Mindful inquiry meditation is specifically for when you want to investigate further your emotions and feelings that may be driving your panic. See what works best for you.

R.A.I.N.

Another informal mindful practice is called R.A.I.N. (origin unknown). This acronym stands for:

* Recognize when a strong emotion or feeling such as panic is present.

* Acknowledge or Allow that it's there.

* Investigate the body, thoughts, and emotions in order to see what you are directly experiencing.

* Non-identify with it, or in other words, don't take it personally.

R.A.I.N. is an insightful and useful self-inquiry practice that you can bring into your daily life to help you discover deeper storylines of what triggers your panicky reactions. You are welcome to bring this simple practice into your life and discover what happens when you make use of it.

Over the next few days or week, bring recognition to any panicky emotions and feelings and allow them to be present in your nonjudgmental awareness. Investigate how they feel in your body and mind. Then make an effort to not identify with them, to not take them so personally. Notice how it feels to not identify with the panicky emotions and feelings. This can be extremely skillful since it helps reduce the storyline dramatically and cultivates the understanding that panicky emotions and feelings are just changing states of mind and are not a complete definition of who you are. In addition, R.A.I.N. may offer you the possibility to look at panic from a perspective that enables you to choose a more constructive response as compared to your old, habitual ways of looking at things.

❋ Karen's Story

Things were closing down fast for Karen while she waited in line at the supermarket one day. Panic began to surge through her body, and she felt as though she was going to faint. Her palms got sweaty, she had a funny taste in her mouth, and she began to breathe very irregularly and rapidly. She realized she was in trouble and needed to do something quickly, before she made a big scene. Fortunately she remembered R.A.I.N. from her mindfulness class and decided to try to put it into practice in this acute panic-stricken situation. She first recognized what was happening and allowed herself to acknowledge that she was panicked. She then investigated the facts with detachment and clarity: just how were her feelings of panic affecting her body, thoughts, and emotions at that moment? After reflecting on this for a few moments, she felt a bit better and began trying to remember what the N in R.A.I.N. stood for. She almost laughed out loud when she remembered. *Duh! Non-identify—don't take it personally.* Afterward, Karen thought, *Wow, that R.A.I.N. practice just saved me from a major panic attack.*

As you deepen your practice of mindfulness with mindful inquiry and R.A.I.N., you will come to know that the very resistance to unacknowledged emotions and feelings associated with panic often causes more panic, more tightness, more pain, more sleeplessness, and more suffering and that by learning to go with the flow, rather than fighting it, you'll discover a whole new world. So why not give it a try? Besides, maybe that story of panic you've been living with isn't the whole picture. Maybe there's another way to live with greater freedom and peace.

By acknowledging your panic and fears, you may open to the possibility of deeper understanding, compassion, and peace. The beautiful poem "Unconditional" by Jennifer Welwood (1998) points to this healing journey.

> Willing to experience aloneness,
> I discover connection everywhere;
> Turning to face my fear,
> I meet the warrior who lives within;
> Opening to my loss,
> I gain the embrace of the universe;
> Surrendering into emptiness,
> I find fullness without end.
> Each condition I flee from pursues me,
> Each condition I welcome transforms me
> And becomes itself transformed
> Into its radiant jewel-like essence.
> I bow to the one who has made it so,
> Who has crafted this Master Game;
> To play it is purest delight—
> To honor its form, true devotion.

Applied Practices

Let's move into some practical applications of mindfulness to help you deal with the rush of panic in your emotions and feelings.

START YOUR
MORNING OFF RIGHT

Have you ever had mornings when the alarm goes off and as your feet touch the ground, a feeling of desperation and panic overtakes your mind? Mornings marred by chronic worry and anxiety can ruin your sense of stability and your entire day. You may experience a nagging feeling that something bad is coming or bad news is on its way. Or you may experience distress about something that happened last week or apprehension about something about to happen in the coming weeks.

Let's have you try out the self-inquiry practice called R.A.I.N., described earlier in this chapter. R.A.I.N. stands for Recognizing your emotions; Acknowledging and Allowing whatever you're feeling; Investigating the body, thoughts, and emotions; and then Not identifying with those feelings. The following version of this practice will teach you ways to cope with your worrisome and anxious feelings or other similarly strong emotions during an episode of panic.

1. Find a place to sit quietly and get into a comfortable position.

2. Focus on your breath. Your breath will guide you into the present moment. If you are holding your breath, take this time to take three deep belly breaths. Pay attention to the flow of the air, the feel of the air, the subtle nuances of the air traveling into and out of your body—starting at your mouth, lips, and nose, then down your throat, into your lungs, and down into your belly. Experience the fullness of

each inhale and exhale. There's no need to rush through this. Each breath is an anchor to being more present.

3. After a few breaths, ask yourself what you are feeling. Are you worried and feeling anxious? Are you feeling distressed about something in the past or fretful about something that may happen in the future? Are you worried about a certain person, place, thing, or occasion? Take this moment to recognize any emotions that come up.

4. After you've explored your feelings, take this moment to allow your feelings to be here with you. Give yourself permission to acknowledge your worries and anxious feelings at this time. Stay in the present moment by tuning in to your breathing. You may be feeling troubled, worrisome, and helpless for a sibling who is ill. You may be feeling anxious about upcoming plans with a friend. This is just how you are feeling right now, and that's okay.

5. You may experience a strong tendency to place judgment on your feelings, such as judging a feeling to be good or bad, right or wrong, fair or unfair. Practice not judging your emotions, not putting labels on them, letting them simply be what they are. Emotions are just emotions, neither good nor bad. Focus on just the facts and return to your breath.

6. Begin to investigate your feelings in your body and mind. Consider where you hold these emotions in your body. Investigate just the facts. How do these feelings affect your body, thoughts, and emotions? Take this time to reflect on what you discover.

7. The last step in your mindful inquiry is non-identifying, or not taking your emotions personally. This may require some effort and practice, since it may feel counterintuitive. Try to remember that you are not your feelings. Your feelings are momentary, passing, impermanent. What you are feeling now may not be what you feel later. By non-identifying, you essentially allow your feelings to be, without making them about you. Your emotions and feelings are a passing state of mind, like a passing train. These emotions that you are feeling now do not identify who you are as a person. Reflect on how you feel when you don't identify with your panicky emotions.

This mindful self-inquiry is an extremely useful tool for shifting your perspective on how you look at panic. Start your mornings in this way to deepen your understanding and soften your reaction to your panicky emotions.

*

RESTORE PEACE IN YOUR HEART

There is no ideal time or place for a panic attack to hit. You may be in the privacy of your home on your day off when panic grips you by the heart. An e-mail, a bill, or a voice message could trigger it. If others are around, you may experience tremendous embarrassment or shame about your panicky feelings. It is intensely uncomfortable to have others, such as family members or roommates, witness your emotional meltdown. Shame is an extremely painful emotion whereby you may even feel apologetic to others for putting them through your panic.

Mindfulness is a way to help you cope with your panicky feelings. Day-to-day chores are an ideal time for bringing mindfulness into your routine at home, at work, at a social gathering at someone's house, or wherever some dirty dishes are piling up. Try this next practice while you wash the dishes, that much-dreaded activity that follows a hard-earned meal.

1. While standing at the sink, close your eyes and take three to five mindful breaths. With each breath, pause and fully experience your inhale and exhale. When you tune in to your breath—its rhythm, pace, sensation, and sound—you drop into the full experience of being present, being here. Now, open your eyes and continue.

2. Turn on the water at the temperature that you desire. While the water is running, keep your fingers in the stream. If you are conscientious about not wasting water, then fill a glass or bowl with water and soak your fingers in it. Notice what you're feeling in the water. How does the water feel against

your skin? What sensations come up? Ask yourself, where does the water come from, beyond the faucet? A mountain, a river, an aqueduct? Consider what a miracle it is to have this free-flowing water at your easy disposal. Take a moment to be grateful for this water.

3. Grab the sponge and add some dish soap. Pay attention to every small detail—the color of the sponge, the smell of the soap, the feel of the bubbles on your hands.

4. Pick up an item to wash and consider where it's been, who used it, and what was eaten or drunk from it. Consider the history or story behind each item—a cup that was a gift from an old friend, dishes from your first marriage, or your child's favorite spoon.

5. Remember to check in often with your breathing and to reconnect with the unfurling present moment.

6. A common challenge that may arise is when difficult emotions start to surface. We all have a natural tendency to push away what feels bad. Take this mindful moment to acknowledge any feelings percolating inside you, and resist the urge to push them away. Allow yourself to simply experience the emotions and let them be there with you. Take note of any subtle fluctuations in the feelings that come into your heart. During times of shame or embarrassment, notice how even these awkward feelings shift—one moment they are intense; the next, barely detectable. Here today, gone tomorrow.

7. Return to the breath as often as you want or need to.

8. As you finish rinsing the dishes and setting them to dry on the rack, or as some dishes head for the dishwasher, pause and be conscious of every movement, every feeling, and everything about this activity and its relationship to you.

For most people, the goal in washing dishes is to get them clean and to be done with it, in order to move on to something else, something more pressing and demanding of their attention. When you bring mindfulness into your daily chores, you experience washing the dishes merely for the sake of washing dishes, without a goal or destination in mind. Mindfully washing the dishes opens you to the experience of fully appreciating and participating in the act and being more aware of the small wonders in life that bring order and calm into your life. During your mindful practice, you are also opening yourself to the awareness that all emotions eventually pass and are never a permanent state of being. Doing routine chores with mindfulness helps train you to bring mindfulness into your approach to strong emotions, such as embarrassment and shame, when they arise. A deeper awareness of these strong feelings will help restore feelings of ease and peacefulness.

*

A GOOD DAY'S WORK

When panic strikes you on the job, it's a challenge to get through your day and to stay focused on your tasks at hand. You may feel as though you have no worth, value, or use. Similarly, you may feel inadequate, deficient, or incompetent. You may feel very alone and isolated when you do not see others expressing these same feelings. But you are not alone. Many people face these same challenging emotions behind closed office doors or as they travel to and from work, suffering in private.

The following mindful breathing practice is for restoring self-kindness and compassion and allowing yourself to befriend your emotions instead of criticizing and judging. There's no time like the present to begin.

1. Find a comfortable place to sit or stand. This is a good time to turn off any devices that may distract you during your practice—cell phone, computer, music, and so on.

2. Focus on your breathing and let yourself be present. Each breath is an opportunity to be in the here and now.

3. Take this pause to examine and investigate what you're feeling. What emotions are stirring? If you are feeling inadequate and undeserving, admit this now. Whatever feelings of not being good enough or ineptitude come to the surface, let them emerge. Allow your emotions to come to the surface and let them be. Let any feelings of panic arise, and then let them take their own path.

4. You may begin to notice that feelings come and go in terms of cycles. All feelings pass, and with your growing awareness of this comes the knowledge that all aspects of life are constantly passing and impermanent, like the stars in the night, like the sun and the moon, like the changing of the tides. There is a secret, hidden comfort in this knowledge of impermanence. Impermanence teaches us to go with the flow of life rather than resisting it.

5. Remember to revisit your breath, returning to the moment of now.

6. Your next step is the practice of self-compassion. Begin by setting your intention for each breath. On each inhale, you may say aloud or to yourself, *I am holding myself with kindheartedness and tenderness.* On each exhale, *I am releasing my self-criticism and self-judgment.* Try this for three to five breaths. Feel free to revise these intentions to reflect what you feel you need and desire from this practice.

7. Notice what you're feeling after this practice. Be tender with yourself and move gently.

Self-kindness may not come easily, particularly during times of panic, which is why we recommend that you make this part of your daily practice of mindfulness. Give yourself the gift of self-compassion and understanding every day.

*

TRANSFORM YOUR ANGER

When something or someone pushes your panic button, you may frequently feel anger. You might carry anger around with you without even being aware that it's there, until it lashes out unpredictably at some moment of contact with another person. You might be face to face, talking on the phone, texting, or e-mailing, when suddenly in a moment of panic, you feel extremely annoyed, infuriated, or offended. These angry emotions get in the way of your ability to communicate effectively and can create a cycle of more inflamed exchanges.

The next time your panic and anger flare up, practice R.A.I.N. as described below. It's a helpful tool for restoring a sense of calm and assisting in difficult conversations when your anger might get in the way of resolution.

1. Start with the breath. Tune in to your breathing and notice what is going on for you right now. You may be breathing shallowly and feeling constraint in your mind and body. Or your breathing may be very rapid and irregular. Take this moment to experience some long, full, slow, deep belly breaths. Pay attention to how air fills your lungs, chest, and stomach on each inhale. Notice how your body deflates on each exhale. Try at least three to five belly breaths.

2. Take this next mindful moment to recognize what is happening. The panic and anger are there, and you acknowledge that this is so.

3. Allow the feelings to emerge. What feelings around your anger come up? Are you stressed, exasperated, tired, or

enraged? Acknowledge whatever feelings are there, without attaching any judgment to them. The feelings are neither positive nor negative, welcome nor unwelcome, wanted nor unwanted.

4. As an experiment, practice beginner's mind (see the Foundation chapter) by imagining, if you can, that you are feeling panic and anger for the first time—that these things are completely new to you. Try to experience being curious about these new emotions. With beginner's mind, you are letting go of your old script for what you know is happening and taking steps toward cultivating a spirit of curiosity about your panicky feelings. Notice what emotions come up while your beginner's-mind cap is on. You might think: *I'm feeling a strange resistance and strong emotional current pulsating in my mind and body. I'm experiencing a flush in my face, and a myriad of fleeting feelings are tumbling out of me. How interesting. Hmm…so this is what anger feels like.*

5. Take another slow, deep belly breath, inhaling and exhaling.

6. Investigate and delve into how your panic and anger feel in your body. Resist any urge to turn away from your feelings as you might have done in the past. Does your anger make you feel hot inside and out? When you're angry and panicky, do you make a fist or tighten some other part of your body? Do you become more easily agitated and feel less understood? Be mindful of how your emotions affect your mind and body.

7. The final step in this exercise is non-identifying. This is the time when you make a conscious effort to not identify with your feelings. They are just feelings, after all, and they do not define who you are as a person. This means basically not taking your feelings personally. These emotions are not about you; they're just feelings that rise and set like the sun and the moon, or like a tornado that stops in for a visit and then leaves again. The feelings come and go. And soon enough, all feelings eventually pass.

Before your anger takes hold of your next conversation, try this mindful practice. You will carry this awareness into your next exchange. The ability to restore your sense of calm using this practice will be a useful communication skill and help you find resolution in every interaction.

*

FREE YOURSELF FROM FEELING OUT OF CONTROL

A great many people who suffer with panic attacks experience feeling as though they are losing control and going crazy. Some people describe feeling a disconnect from reality that scares and confuses them. You may feel completely helpless, as though there is nothing you can do and no one can help you. You literally believe that a threat is present, likely, or imminent. It's a frightening experience that is not soon forgotten. In fact, the fear alone that it may happen again is enough to start the cycle of panic and insecurity. If you're feeling scared or insecure about a reoccurrence right now, you are not alone and there is help.

There's no predicting when your next panic attack will occur. It might happen while you're out running errands, interacting with strangers at the market or post office. Being in public may feel like the worst-case scenario for a panic attack, but it is also your cue to listen to your mind and body. This next practice uses mindful inquiry. It will help you investigate what is driving or fueling your panicky emotions in order that you might become freer from them. Practice these skills during an episode of panic on an occasion when you're out and about.

1. Before you begin, ask yourself whether this is a good time to explore your feelings. Do you feel safe at this time? If you do feel safe, proceed with the next step. If you do not feel safe, then it is okay to wait and attempt this practice at a more convenient time, perhaps when you've returned to the privacy of your home.

2. Wherever you are—running around town, meeting up with a friend, standing in line, or walking down the aisle of a market—your practice begins as soon as you tune in to and stay with your breathing. You carry your breath everywhere, and it is your focal point for maintaining your connection to the present wherever you go. Be mindful of your breathing, in and out, noticing the sensations of warmth and coolness, the rise and fall, the in and out of each breath.

3. Take this moment to recognize any and all feelings that are with you now. If you feel out of control, then just acknowledge it as a feeling, without attaching details or stories behind it. If you feel an uncontrollable fear that you're going insane, then recognize this feeling without striving to critique or analyze the feeling. Give yourself permission to just identify the emotions that are coming up and let them be. You may be telling yourself: *I feel as if something horrible is about to happen. I feel as though I've lost touch with reality. I feel as though I can't trust anyone. Maybe I can't even trust myself.* Other unrelated feelings and thoughts may come to mind, like *I'm hungry. I hope that he calls soon. I wonder where I left my to-do list.* Make space in this moment to simply let these feelings emerge, and try to stay with the feelings and thoughts. Simply notice what's here, without attaching yourself or clinging to any one thought or feeling.

4. You may experience a strong impulse to resist or fight against these painful and terrifying emotions, as may be your habit. We all have a natural tendency to strive toward what feels good. For this exercise, you are practicing nonstriving: not trying, or not attempting to change your

feelings or shift them in a different direction. Just let the feelings be what they are. The less energy you spend trying to resist or alter your panicky emotions, the lesser the hold your panic can have on you.

5. Remember to be aware of your breathing and to connect again with the here and now.

With practice, you will come to learn what is driving your feelings and to let them run their natural course. Strong emotions can be fierce and unrelenting for a time, but eventually they fade and you move on.

*

WORK THROUGH
PAINFUL EMOTIONS

Panic and sadness go hand in hand for many people. Panic is not easily fixed, and it can leave you feeling depressed, desperate, alone, and unable to cope with even small problems. You may find yourself crying at the slightest provocation and without warning. Long after a panic attack has diminished, you may experience a clinging sorrow and heavy-heartedness throughout your mind and body. By the time you return home for what you hope to be a peaceful evening with your family or roommates, making dinner and watching TV, your misery may be telling you to isolate yourself in your room and forget about everything else.

R.A.I.N. can teach you to embrace your sadness in order to understand your panic and sadness from another viewpoint. You can practice R.A.I.N. while eating dinner or while watching your favorite TV programs. It is useful to bring mindfulness into your life, however briefly, even when life is bubbling all around you, brimming with activity.

1. Once you're ready to begin, center on your breathing. Notice the oscillation between air moving into and air moving out of your body. In and out.

2. Take this pause to recognize any intense emotions or feelings that come up. By recognizing, you are just identifying the feelings and making a note of them. You may think to yourself: *I feel depressed. I feel misunderstood. I feel utterly sad and empty.*

3. Acknowledge these emotions by allowing them to be here with you. Perhaps you might envision your feelings of sadness or desperation sitting beside you, like a couple of very close friends. Your feelings of sorrow are with you but they are separate, outside of you, accompanying you on your path through life.

4. Return to your breathing and being present.

5. You may experience some doubt along the way in your practice. This is perfectly normal. Doubt will try to sabotage your practice and convince you that nothing can help you through your sorrow and panic. Doubt may say to you: *This meditation won't work. Nothing works, so why bother?* The best prescription for doubt is to just be aware of your doubt. When you notice and acknowledge your doubt, you can begin to take back your confidence and move ahead. By identifying your doubt, you can add doubt to your row of emotional friends seated with you. Allow your disbelief to just hang around if it wants to. Doubt is just another companion who likes to tag along for the ride.

6. Now it's time to investigate how the sadness feels in your mind and body. Where is the sadness coming from? Where does your sadness like to hide out? Be patient and be aware of any feelings that arise.

7. The final step is to not take your feelings personally and to not identify with your sadness. You are you, and your emotions are just emotions. Remember, your feelings are just

close friends who come and go. Some feelings may sit and stay for a bit, while others may drop in for only a quick visit. Eventually, each one leaves. How does it feel to not identify with your panicky and sorrowful emotions?

8. As you return to your dinner and interactions with others or your program, take a mindful moment to be fully present with yourself and others.

This practice offers you a chance to form a new perspective and choose a more constructive response to your panic rather than the old, familiar way of withdrawing from your painful and despairing emotions.

*

LET EMOTIONS BE

Another common feeling for people who struggle with panic is overwhelming fear, alarm, and apprehension. You may fear something from your past or something that might happen in the future. You may fear being out of control, and when a panic attack strikes, you may fear that it will never end. As soon as one panic attack has passed, you may live in constant fear of another attack. Your fear is normal, but you might be surprised at how powerful the practice of mindfulness can be for changing your response to these frightening emotions that accompany panic. This next mindful practice will assist you with acknowledging troubling feelings and letting them be while doing chores at home, such as folding laundry.

1. Start by checking in with your breath. Even as you get stationed with piles of laundry stretched in front of you, tune in to your breathing and connect with this present moment right now.

2. Feel free to set your intentions for this practice, such as *May this practice bring me more awareness. May this practice enhance my self-compassion and understanding when I am feeling afraid and overwhelmed.*

3. While you fold your laundry, take this time to really be conscious of every detail about the laundry. Are the clothes fresh from the dryer and still warm? Who was wearing these clothes or sleeping on them or using these items last? Notice

the colors, the sizes, the variety, the worn spots, and so on. With tenderness and sensitivity, acknowledge any feelings that arise as you fold your laundry.

4. Acknowledge any fears that spring to mind. Are you fearful of someone seeing you have a panic attack? Are you scared of a future attack? Are you apprehensive and anxious about leaving the house for fear of something going wrong? Take this pause to recognize all the emotions that come up. Practice folding each fear into an article of laundry that you're folding. Place each fear on top of the other, as if making a pile of fears out of your laundry. These fears are with you, but they don't own you. They exist, but they don't make up who you are. They are just fears.

5. Check in again with your breathing and connect with the present.

6. Finally, let your feelings of fear and apprehension just be. This is not the same thing as letting go. If you've ever tried to let go of your panic, it probably didn't work. If letting go was so easy, you'd have mastered your panic by now. Letting be means not putting any effort into changing or control-ling your feelings. Your feelings are here with you, piled up in the folded laundry before you. There they sit. And the next time you fold laundry, you will likely have a whole new set of articles to fold and a whole new list of emotions and fears and apprehensions waiting for you to pay attention to. The feelings will change as often as the laundry changes, as often as the weather changes.

Letting your emotions run their course is one of the greatest gifts that you can give yourself. In time, you will become more and more familiar with the passing and changing of your emotions, and you will learn to go with the flow of your feelings without needing to control or change anything. May you experience more peace and contentment with each passing breath.

*

GET THE REST YOU NEED

Panic attacks are one of the most frightening emotional experiences in life. It's difficult to describe the disabling sense of extreme terror and the intense psychological distress that overcome you in the midst of a panic attack. Some people say that they feel paralyzed with terror. Others describe a sensation of choking or being smothered. One woman described feeling as though her heart would burst or explode in her chest. If you experience panic before bed at night, then you may also face disrupted sleep or no sleep at all.

The following application of R.A.I.N. will help you relax and get the rest that you need each night. Like any exercise in self-inquiry, to be truly beneficial, it takes regular practice, incorporating each step into your nightly routine.

1. You may sit up in bed or lie down—it doesn't matter, as long as you are fully alert and comfortable.

2. Become aware of your breathing. This is the first step in aligning with the present moment, living in the now. Each conscious breath is your bridge to a deeper connection with being more present. You may be more accustomed to experiencing your life with a focus on the past or the future, but for this moment you are consciously focusing on what is happening right here and now.

3. When you are in the throes of panicky emotions, it is difficult to unwind from the terror. Take this moment to set your intentions for what you would like to walk away with from this practice, such as *May this practice restore my belief*

in my own capacity to heal. May this practice help me live with more ease in my body and mind. May it teach me to have greater self-compassion, kindness, and gentleness.

4. Begin to recognize whatever powerful or severe emotions come up. Envision your feelings as leaves on a tree...each feeling fluttering on a branch, asking to be seen and heard and paid attention to.

5. Acknowledge and allow your feelings. You may say: *I feel scared and panicky. I feel terrified and full of dread. I feel stressed about every little thing in my life.* Again, imagine each of your feelings as a leaf on a windy day. Some leaves, like feelings, will cling tightly to the branch, and others will spin and flutter about. Allow each feeling to move freely and dance around. You might say to yourself: *Oh look, there's terror, gripping the highest branch overhead. And oh look, there's manic distress, swirling wildly around and around the base of the tree.* Simply observe each feeling, one at a time.

6. Now take this pause to investigate your feelings in your mind and body and see what's really going on. What are you experiencing directly? What are the facts here in your situation?

7. Remember to be aware of your breathing from time to time, paying mindful attention to the flow of air into and out of your body.

8. The final step is non-identification, or not taking your feelings personally. Your feelings of terror and immense fear are just feelings. These feelings cannot define who you are or

your purpose in life. You are not the feelings that come and go, just as you are not the leaves on the tree that come and go and change with the seasons.

9.   Check in again with your breathing and your awareness of being present. How are you feeling now? Do you notice a shift in your mind and body?

When you mindfully observe your feelings, you can loosen the grip that panic and terror have on your life. Mindfulness is a powerful tool for reviving your sense of ease and deepening your self-compassion for a more restful night ahead.

*

Here We Are

In this chapter you have been introduced to mindful inquiry meditation and the R.A.I.N. mindful practice as a way to deal with panic in your emotions and feelings. You also explored and practiced some ways that you can bring mindfulness into different parts of your life. We recommend that you informally practice mindfulness every day, bringing mindfulness into your daily life as suggested, and also continue to practice S.T.O.P. from the previous chapter. In the next chapter you'll investigate how mindfulness works to help you deal with the rush of panic in your thoughts.

chapter 3

Calming the Rush of Panic in Your Thoughts

In the Foundation chapter you learned about mindfulness in both its formal and informal practices. In chapter 1, you worked with feelings of panic in the body and learned the foundational MBSR meditations of mindful breathing and the body scan, as well as the S.T.O.P. practice. In chapter 2, you explored dealing with panic-filled emotions and feelings using mindful inquiry meditation and the R.A.I.N. practice. In this chapter we will introduce you to sitting meditation and the "Pause, Observe/Experience, and Allow" practice for working with thoughts related to panic.

When your mind is occupied with panicky thoughts, you may feel as if they'll never stop. You may feel like you're losing control, you're going crazy, or you're going to die. This type of thinking is called "catastrophic thinking," and it can spin you down a spiral of despair to a place where you feel over-whelmed and paralyzed. Through sitting meditation you will gradually deepen your understanding of the nature of change in your breath, senses, and states of mind and learn how to deal better with panic, distress, and the other "ten thousand" sufferings of life. Your perspective will widen. This understanding will help you loosen the grip of panic, because you will see panic-stricken thoughts to be just as transient as bodily sensations or feelings and emotions. Sitting meditation will help further your understanding of non-identification, which we introduced in the R.A.I.N. practice in chapter 2. Both of these mindful practices will help you keep your thoughts—rumination, anticipation of future panic attacks, "what if" thinking, and habitual thought patterns—from fueling panic. We will investigate this deeply because this is an important catalyst for living a life with less panic and more ease of being.

Sitting Meditation

Sitting meditation is a blended practice that consists of bringing your awareness to five objects of meditation, progressively: (1) the breath, (2) physical sensations, (3) sounds, (4) mind states, and (5) choiceless or present-moment awareness. This meditation teaches you that no matter what you bring your attention to, you can experience directly the impersonal or ownerless nature of change. What we mean by the impersonal or ownerless nature of change is that your physical sensations, other senses, and mind states—meaning your thoughts and emotions—are ceaselessly changing and that you don't have much control over them. You will come to realize, for example, that you can work on living a healthy life, but you cannot prevent illness, aging, or death; these things happen regardless of your intentions for them not to happen.

As you see more clearly into the workings of your mind and body, you'll also begin to see old, habitual, reactive thought patterns that are fueled by the stories you tell yourself and identify with. With this growing understanding, you can learn to see, from your own direct experience, a wider perspective and not be held to self-limiting definitions of yourself that don't serve your health and well-being. You can make choices to live much better in the midst of panic, stress, imperfection, and dissatisfaction.

Let's take a look at the five objects of sitting meditation.

Mindfulness of Breathing

Sitting meditation begins with mindful breathing. In this particular meditation you continue to be mindful of the breath, as introduced in chapter 1, but then we bring in a new emphasis by asking you to be mindful of the changing nature of the breath as it ebbs and flows. The breath comes in and the breath goes out—just like the tides. As you begin to understand how everything changes in life, you can begin to learn to go with the flow of life rather than fighting it.

> *Take a pause right now and bring awareness to your breath and experience its changing nature.*

Mindfulness of Sensations

From the mindful breathing practice you gently shift your focus to mindfulness of physical sensations, bringing awareness now into the body and becoming mindful of whatever distinct or

105

predominant sensations you're feeling in each unfolding moment. Just as you were mindful of the breath coming in and going out, you now bring awareness to sensations and experience that they are also changing. There are itches, aches, pains, tingles, warmth, coolness, dryness, wetness, and so many different sensations appearing and disappearing. These sensations are arising and passing away of their own accord. They're not under any kind of ownership or direction—they're just impermanent sensations, revealing the nature of change.

Take a pause right now and bring awareness to sensations in your body and feel how they're constantly changing.

Mindfulness of Sounds

Next, you'll extend your mindful awareness to sounds (also known as hearing meditation). As you bring nonjudgmental awareness to sounds, to the world of audibility, you will also come in direct contact again with the nature of change. There's no need to like or dislike the sounds you hear; just listen to them arising and then fading away. They appear of their own accord and leave of their own accord. Like sensations, they are without an owner—they're just sound waves rising and passing away.

Mindfulness of sounds can be very useful and practical for those of us who live in a noisy world. Consider the sounds you hear to be just sound waves teaching you to go with the flow of life. As your understanding of change begins to deepen, you may begin to realize that panic is just another happening that has its own time: it comes and goes. Nothing stays the same.

*Take a pause right now and bring awareness to sounds and
listen to all the different sounds ever changing.*

Mindfulness of Mind States

After meditating on sounds, you'll shift to mind states that
pertain to thoughts and emotions as the object of your meditation. Mindfulness cultivates your ability to bring awareness to
thoughts and emotions as they arise, develop, and recede.
Thoughts and emotions are just mental events that come and go
like clouds in the sky. Rather than getting involved with the
contents of your thoughts and emotions, just let them be. In
time, you will come to recognize that these mind states are just
as ephemeral as the sounds you were listening to, the sensations
you were feeling, and the breath you were breathing. You will
begin to experience that all these states of mind come and go of
their own accord. As you practice non-identification with your
mind states, you'll begin to see that your mind has a mind of its
own and is also without an owner. So many thoughts, emotions,
fantasies, moments of panic, planning, memories, dreams, and
countless mind states are perennially arising and passing away.

When you learn and practice non-identification with panic,
you'll feel more at ease in your life. It is said that the mind is the
creator of its own heavens and its own hells. The mind is home
to our thought processes, and with its perceptions we create our
world. When panic occupies and consumes our thoughts, it can
take over and hold us hostage. Panicky thoughts race and swirl
about, and the common result is feeling overwhelmed by a sense

of impending doom. These thoughts may send us to the emergency room believing that we're having a heart attack. These thoughts can paralyze us so much that we are unable to get out of the house. These thoughts can make us break out in a cold sweat and begin to hyperventilate just before we give a speech.

As a way to work with panic, perhaps this metaphor will be helpful: As you learn to sit back and just experience the coming and going of your mind states, you can be like the sky giving space to a storm. It is the virtue of the sky, which is made of air, to give as much space as a storm needs—and in the end, as a result of having that space, the storm eventually dissipates. In the same vein, as you give space to the storms of panic, acknowledging what's present in the body and mind and letting it be, it too will gradually dissipate, recede, or fade away.

Stormy mind states are here for a while and then they leave. Where they came from and where they go is often difficult to comprehend, but what's most important is to know that they are here and that they are governed by the laws of change

When you practice mindfulness, you will begin to understand yourself more deeply. You will learn to recognize dysfunctional patterns within you that don't serve your health and well-being. These insights will help release you from old embedded habits—what we call your conditioning—to help free you from the snares of panic.

As you become aware of the stories you spin and the traps you create, you can begin to disengage from them. You'll come to understand that panic is just another impersonal state of mind that comes and goes; that these thoughts are not facts, nor are they a complete definition of who you are. Freeing yourself from your own self-limiting constructions of yourself will bring deeper levels of freedom and peace. Once you become aware of the stories you spin and the traps you find yourself in, you can then begin to disengage from them. You may realize that your story, your running narrative, doesn't serve your health and well-being.

Take a pause right now and bring awareness to mind states and experience how they're ceaselessly changing—just states of mind.

Choiceless Awareness

The last object we introduce in sitting meditation is called choiceless or present-moment awareness. In this phase of sitting meditation, you become aware of whatever's arising in the present moment. Rather than focusing solely on one object, as with the breath, sensation, sounds, or mind states, you now open up your awareness to whatever's prominent and distinct in the unfolding of each present moment in your body or mind.

Just as you might sit by the side of a stream and watch whatever goes downstream, in choiceless awareness you sit in the present moment and experience whatever's there, whatever's prominent and distinct. Choiceless awareness is the most fluid of mindful practices that's reflective of moment-to-moment changing experience. You begin to see clearly into the body and mind as a dynamic organism in a state of constant change. Although outwardly you may be sitting motionless—visibly unchanging—inwardly it's another story. There are sounds to be heard, sensations to be felt, thoughts and emotions to be experienced, and the breath coming in and going out. Sitting meditation teaches you how to ride the waves of panic knowing that it won't last forever. Panic is just a passing mind state.

Take a pause right now and bring awareness to the present moment, to whatever's prominent in your body or mind, and experience its changing nature.

FOUNDATIONAL PRACTICE:
Sitting Meditation

Take a seat on a cushion or chair and find a position in which you can be alert and comfortable. If you prefer to lie down on the bed or carpet, you are welcome to do so.

Similar to other meditations, choose a quiet environment where you will not be interrupted. Turn off your phone or any other electronic device that could disturb you. Read and practice the script for this guided meditation below, pausing after each paragraph for a short time, or feel free to download a recording from New Harbinger Publications at newharbinger. com/25264. You can download a fifteen-, thirty-, or forty-five-minute version.

Begin by congratulating yourself that you are dedicating some time to meditation.

As you become present, become aware of the body and mind and whatever's being felt within your body and mind—checking in with how you are feeling from the day's happenings or whatever has been going on within you recently.

Simply allow and acknowledge whatever is present and let it be, without any form of problem solving or evaluation.

Gently, shift the focus to mindful breathing. As you breathe in, be aware of breathing in, and as you breathe out, be aware of breathing out, breathing normally and naturally. Being aware of breathing and focusing on either the tip of the nose or the abdomen. If focusing on the tip of the nose, feel the touch of the air as you breathe in and out. If focusing on the belly, feel the belly expanding with each inhalation and contracting with each exhalation.

Just living your life one inhalation and one exhalation at a time. Breathing in, breathing out, experiencing each breath appear and disappear. Just breathing. Just like the waves of the sea ebb and flow, so too the breath comes and goes out, revealing the nature of change.

Now gently withdraw from the breath and bring your awareness into the world of sensations in the body. Experiencing, feeling, and acknowledging the varying sensations as they change from moment to moment and letting them be.

As you sense into the body, you may find areas of tension and tightness. If you can allow them to soften and relax, that is fine. If not, just let them be.

Riding the waves of sensation with your awareness, allowing them to flow wherever they need to go. In time you will also directly experience how sensations rise and pass away, just as the breath comes in and goes out, disclosing the changing nature of things.

Now release awareness of sensations and bring your attention to sounds, to hearing meditation, listening to all the sounds appearing and disappearing in your environment. Being aware of the multitude of varying sounds either in the room or outside. You can also bring awareness to sounds in your body such as your pulse, your heartbeat, or a ringing in the ears, from one moment into the next.

Whether the sounds are external or internal, notice how they are ever changing, just like the sensations and the breath. Sounds rise; sounds pass away. Listening to them coming and gradually going...they are just sounds.

Now gently shift your attention from awareness of sounds to mind states—thoughts and emotions—and experience the mind without any aversion or indulgence. Just acknowledging the multitude of varying mental formations from moment to moment.

Like lying on a field and watching the clouds float by...experiencing the mind in the same way...mind states coming and mind states going, disclosing this nature of change.

You may become aware that the mind has a mind of its own. It analyzes, scrutinizes, plans, remembers, compares, and contrasts; it dreams and fantasizes; it likes and dislikes. The mind is busy thinking about this and that, thoughts rising and falling. Experiencing them appear and disappear...just thoughts without ownership...they just come and go.

Cultivating awareness to be like a meteorologist, experiencing the internal weather systems of the mind without judgment, simply being with the way things are...thoughts rise, thoughts fall...experiencing them appear and disappear...they are just impersonal thought formations.

As you learn to give space to whatever is arising with greater equanimity and balance, you can begin to go with the flow. Instead of putting your energy into resisting what is there, just go with it... they are just mind states rising and passing, ever changing.

Even if you are experiencing storms of panic, just give the storm space and it will gradually diminish.

Very gently now, withdraw awareness from your mind states and bring your attention to the present moment itself as the primary object of attention; this is called choiceless or present-moment awareness.

Choiceless awareness is the practice of being mindful of whatever arises in the present moment, in the body and in the mind, whether that is the breath, sounds, sensations, or mind states. Just sit back and experience the show of the ever-shifting tides of the body and mind. Although very still on the outside, on the inside may be another story. Your body and mind form a dynamic organism interacting with constantly changing stimuli from the senses and the mind.

Be mindful and experience whatever is predominant or distinct in the body and mind, and be present to it. If nothing is particularly compelling and you are unsure of where to focus your attention, you can always go back to the breath to fasten onto the here and now.

This is similar to sitting in or by a stream and just experiencing whatever goes downstream. Sometimes there are breaths, sounds, or sensations; sometimes there are thoughts and emotions. Sit and experience directly the changing nature of the body and mind.

Even if you are experiencing storms of panic, worry, angst, or painful memories, allow them to be there. Let them pass through your awareness. You will see and experience that they will gradually diminish.

Now withdraw from choiceless awareness and come back to the breath, feeling your whole body from head to toe to fingertip as you breathe in and out. Feeling the whole of the body rising on an inhalation and falling on an exhalation.

Feeling the body as a whole organism, unified, connected, and whole.

May you again congratulate yourself for practicing this meditation that is a contribution to your health and well-being.

May all beings dwell with peace.

*

How to Practice Sitting Meditation

Practice sitting meditation once a day. You may want to work with it for the next week and see how it goes. This is the best way to bring it into your life. Make time to do sitting meditation when you can—even a short period of meditation will give you benefit. As mentioned before, find a time that works best for you, and since everyone is different, whatever time you do it is the best time. Let this be a practice you look forward to, a gift to yourself as a way to become more balanced within your body and mind. Feel free to use an alarm clock or timer.

❋ *Susan's Story*

Susan lived with panic around the fact that she was getting married soon. We had a few sessions of sitting meditation together, with her being mindful of what was coming up in her body and mind. While meditating she noticed a feeling that she wasn't good enough, and this caused her to feel anxious. The anxiety at first seemed to settle in her neck and then turned into a huge knot in her belly, and she felt more panicked by it. She continued, however, to be mindful and acknowledged those feelings and let them be to see where they would take her. She began to witness that in time they dissipated and left—without her even intentionally trying to push them away. They seemed to arise on their own and leave on their own—like an uninvited guest, they appeared and then left unannounced. As Susan stayed with this process, she realized how fleeting these panicky mind states were and that she didn't have to take them on as a permanent truth.

Interestingly enough, as she stayed with the panic, experiencing it coming and going and not identifying with it, she actually had an insight. She remembered that at an early age, she had been criticized about her homework by both her parents and her schoolteacher—it was a double whammy. Susan internalized that all of her original work was not adequate and that she was only okay when her parents or her teacher corrected her work. This of course affected her self-worth and self-esteem. She realized that her panic around getting married was a result of thinking that maybe her husband would find out that she really wasn't good enough.

After Susan understood what she had done to herself, her self-worth and self-esteem deepened and her panic left. That story of her being unworthy was just a passing mind state and not a definition of who she was. She was becoming at peace with her original and unique self! She did indeed get married, and her marriage flourished.

Pause, Observe/Experience, and Allow

We would like to introduce you to another way to informally practice mindfulness, called "Pause, Observe/Experience, and

Allow." This is akin to S.T.O.P. (chapter 1) and R.A.I.N. (chapter 2), with a bit of a twist. We feel that it's important for you to have a number of meditations and mindful practices that you can draw from and work with. We understand that for some of you, one particular meditation or informal practice may be very helpful while another may be less so. Yet bear in mind that things change, so what may not be that useful to you now may be more useful in the future.

"Pause, Observe/Experience, and Allow" can help you work through panicky thoughts and events so that you don't get so deeply caught up in them. You definitely know that getting sucked into panic is not where you want to go. Fortunately you've been learning practices to help you get unstuck. "Pause, Observe/Experience, and Allow" offers you yet another tool for dealing with panic.

Just as you have been mindful of mind states in sitting meditation, experiencing how they come and go on their own and learning to not take them so personally, you can bring this same perspective into your everyday life. Wherever you are—at the post office, at the bank, at the office, or at home—you can practice dealing with moments of panic as they arise by using "Pause, Observe/Experience, and Allow." When you notice the rush of panic emerging, take a moment to breathe from your belly and *pause* to become present. *Observe and experience* your body sensations, thoughts, and emotions, and then *allow* them to be, giving space for them to go wherever they need to go. See what happens when you bring the practice of "Pause, Observe/Experience, and Allow" into a panicky moment.

We would like to invite you to reflect upon the fact that life is indeed made of moments, and although a moment of panic may seem like a thousand years, in actuality it's not very long.

Like all events in the body and mind, whatever arises, passes—for all things are certain to change.

By practicing "Pause, Observe/Experience, and Allow," you can begin to watch the storms of panic come and go and gradually feel less affected by them. You are learning to give space to the storm of panic by not reacting to it. You are learning to pause, observe/experience, and allow the panicky feelings to go wherever they need to go. When you give space to the storm of panic, eventually the storm dissipates.

You will come to see these mind and body states of panic as impersonal formations that are always changing. When you become less reactive and regard these panicky events as transient, you will become not so enslaved by them. In time, you'll experience deeper levels of freedom and peace.

Practicing "Pause, Observe/Experience, and Allow" builds your ability to step back and be with the body and mind. A mountain is a wonderful example from nature that shows us how to live with greater balance and ease. Just as a mountain is steady and grounded in the midst of changing weather day in and day out, you can learn to sit in more balance with the weather systems of your body and mind.

✳ *Frank's Story*

Frank, an inventor, had come up with some new medical devices for use in life-saving heart surgery. When he started a business to get these inventions into the hands of doctors, he had to deal with experiencing panic at times. At the office—on his own turf and in control of his environment—he was fine and things went fairly well, but when he had to travel to sell and support the use of his devices, it was another story.

Because he had so much panic, Frank would have liked to have someone else in charge of sales for his business, but he couldn't afford to hire the right professional just yet, and those who might be interested in helping him didn't have enough of a technological background. As a result, Frank needed to make sales presentations himself, as well as thoroughly explain to the surgeons how to use his devices, which often meant accompanying them into surgery to consult with them on how best to implant and use them.

Just the thought of walking into the surgery was enough to make Frank's hands sweaty and his breathing rapid and irregular. He knew that he desperately needed to learn to calm down his panic so that he could successfully market his devices and see them put to good use. The last thing he wanted was to have a full-blown panic attack in the operating room.

Frank became proactive and took a mindfulness class, where he learned various formal meditations and informal practices that helped him a lot. Mindful belly breathing was one of his favorites since it helped him regulate his breath and come back into balance. Frank also related with the notion from sitting meditation that we are not our thoughts, but most of all he connected with "Pause, Observe/Experience, and Allow." This was incredibly helpful for him, in conjunction with mindful breathing in everyday situations. Whenever he thought about going out to see the surgeon or when he was about to go into the operating room, Frank would take a breath in and out to pause. This opened up a space for him to observe in a matter-of-fact way just what he was experiencing physically, mentally, and emotionally. Frank then began to allow and acknowledge what he was feeling and began to let things be. In time, those panicky feelings subsided and dissipated, and Frank felt great relief, release, and happiness by learning how to face and transform his panic.

Applied Practices

Let's move into some mindful practices for dealing with the rush of panic in your thoughts.

RELAX ABOUT
SOCIAL SITUATIONS

Say you've been invited to a close friend's party or perhaps an obligatory work-related social gathering. You may desire to go or you may not, but you don't want to leave the safety of your home. In fact, the very thought of stepping outside your door or being away from home is enough to set off a panic attack. Your mind is racing with jumbled, irrational, and anxious thoughts. Your panic might be further fueled by worrisome and intrusive "what if" thinking, such as *What if I don't know anyone at the party? What if I have a panic attack when I get there? What if something happens to me on the way to the party?* If the shackle of the fear of being away from home is strong enough, your panic might win out and you may miss out on the gathering.

You don't have to live this way. The "Pause, Observe/Experience, and Allow" practice will help free you from the clutches of your panic and fearfulness by giving you a new perspective and the space to ride out the storm of panic until it scatters or dissolves.

1. While you're still at home, or sitting in your car outside of the party, or even during the throes of a panic attack at the party, find a comfortable place to sit, bringing your attention to your posture, and pause. You should be sitting tall, fully supported and alert.

2. Begin with a few belly breaths. You might want to put your hand directly on your stomach in order to focus on the rise and fall of this region specifically. After a few breaths, what

do you notice about your breathing? Take this mindful time to pause and be with the next three to five breaths.

3. Set your intentions for this practice and what you would like to learn from it. You may say aloud or to yourself: *May this practice help me deepen my self-compassion for my panicky thoughts and feelings. May it open my perspective and free me from this fear. May it give me the strength I need to leave my home and attend this gathering.* Feel free to make up your own intentions that best suit your situation.

4. Again, reconnect with your breath and anchor yourself in the unfolding present moment.

5. Observe and experience each panic-ridden thought, feeling, and sensation by simply witnessing whatever crops up, without attaching any value to it. Each time a thought replays itself, simply acknowledge the thought for just what it is, a thought. It might be good or it might be bad—who really can say? Thoughts are just thoughts. Your thoughts say nothing about who you are or how you define your life. Don't give the thoughts more significance than they deserve.

6. As thoughts, feelings, and sensations continue to emerge, notice where they go and what happens to them. Do some thoughts stick around and repeat themselves over and over? Do other thoughts appear and disappear swiftly? Do you find new thoughts and feelings issuing forth and then moving along? You might liken your mental experience to watching cars on a highway, where each thought or feeling

is a car. At times, a flood of thoughts and feelings causes gridlock. Later, traffic eases up and fewer thoughts and feelings are on the road. After some time passes, only a few thoughts and feelings remain, speeding along, quickly passing out of sight and out of mind.

7. Allow these thoughts and feelings to just be here with you, without judgment or debate. Simply listen, and allow all the responses that reveal themselves. Remember to meet any feelings with compassion and kindness. Offer them mercy and healing. Stay open to the wisdom that may present itself from this reflection.

You may find the highway metaphor useful for observing and allowing your panicky moments to run their natural course. May you move gently and enjoy the connections that you make at the party.

*

OVERCOME YOUR FEAR OF CROWDS OR TIGHT SPACES

If you fear crowds and open spaces, then something as ordinary as going to a school, a bank, or even a movie can activate your panic. At the other end of the spectrum is the fear of enclosed spaces, such as a crowded room, bus, airplane, or elevator. Whichever situation you fear, sometimes the greater fear is the fear of having a panic attack in this situation. Panic is often driven by anticipation of what *could* happen. Since you must leave your home at some point, you will likely be confronted with many of these locales, possibly more than one in the same day. You cannot avoid these places, so you live with the dread that what has happened in the past will likely happen again. So what can you do when your panic gets provoked?

This next mindful meditation will help you pause, observe/experience, and allow in order to step back and watch your mind and body. With regular practice, you will learn how to live with more balance and ease wherever you go and no matter how severe your panicky thoughts are.

1. Depending on where you are during your panic attack, take this mindful moment to find a place to sit down or stand with comfort. Don't worry about feeling self-conscious during this exercise if other people are around. They will not notice what you are doing.

2. In this moment of pause, take a few belly breaths, summoning air into your body, feeling your rib cage open and your belly expand on the inhale and completely releasing the air

from your body on the exhale, feeling your chest and belly gently collapse.

3. Set your intentions for this practice. You may say aloud or to yourself: *May this practice teach me that I am my own resource for healing. May it help me cultivate greater balance and ease in my mind and body.*

4. Check in with yourself and notice what's going on for you. What thoughts are popping up?

5. Observe and experience as a matter of fact each thought. You may be thinking: *This keeps happening to me. I can't go anywhere without my panic attacks flaring up. Soon, there will be no place I can go where I feel safe.*

6. Remember to breathe and reconnect with the present moment.

7. Allow and acknowledge whatever comes to mind and let it be. Take this moment to let your fears and panicky thoughts be, and just step back and watch. Allow your thoughts to focus on what you are doing now or where you are now, as if you were a filmmaker watching and observing his or her final project. You are taking in the script, the details of your life, and the cinematography. There are highs and lows, intense and subdued parts—a constant changing of various worrisome and anxious thoughts, coming and going.

8. You may notice a tendency to get stuck sorting through thoughts from the past or the future. If you find yourself anticipating distress, calculating your escape, checking your

watch obsessively, or thinking about past mistakes or "failures," your anxious thoughts will intensify. When this happens, try to stay in the now, and your panicky thoughts will settle down. Do what you can to return your focus to your immediate surroundings and your breath. You may notice people having a conversation nearby, or the texture of the carpet, or the colors in a poster.

9. Tell yourself: *I am staying in the here and now. My feet are on the floor. My thoughts live inside my mind. My mind lives inside my body. I will deal with whatever comes up when it occurs and when that time comes.*

The power of letting be is in your growing awareness of the impermanence of all that is—every fear, every thought, every sensation. Everything is in motion. Like the programs on TV in which eventually there is a break for commercials, gradually your panic will take a break and disappear. And in this awareness you will find the greatest relief and calm from your panic.

*

COPE WITH YOUR
FEAR OF ILLNESS

We call them the "what ifs." If you're experiencing a fear of illness, your panicky thoughts might sound like this: *What if I get sick? What if I forget my medicine? What if the pharmacy is out of my prescription? What if I never feel well again?* "What if" thinking is common, and yet it's scary and disturbing because these things might just happen. Unfortunately, future thinking is a mind trap, because there's always something bad that could happen—your mind can always find something to worry about. Combine "what if" thinking with a fear of being seriously sick and you may find your anxious thoughts reeling out of control. You may have already called your doctor and scheduled an appointment.

The following mindful practice—a version of "Pause, Observe/Experience, and Allow"—is easy to do anywhere. It will help you calm the rush of panic and loosen the grip of those nagging and incessant "what if" thoughts. Try it now.

1. Take this moment to pause and put everything on hold for just a brief moment. Take several breaths in and out during this pause. Remember to return to your breathing every time you start to drift away from the present moment.

2. Observe and experience any and all thoughts, feelings, and sensations that are taking place right now. If you are being overrun by "what if" thinking, simply notice that your thoughts are just thoughts and that they're constantly changing like the weather. For example, you may think:

What if my child gets exposed to the flu bug that's going around? Maybe I should take more vitamin C today. What if I'm all out of vitamin C? Thoughts eventually dissolve and are followed by more thoughts, which also eventually dissolve.

3. You may notice some doubt arise during this practice. Doubt is a normal challenge that tries to convince you that a practice can't help you or that it won't work because the panic is too strong. When you hear this voice of doubt, simply be aware of it and acknowledge it just like the other thoughts and feelings that you have. Consider introducing yourself to your doubt. You might say silently: *Hello, Mr. Doubt. I see you over there, shaking your head with skepticism and suspicion. You're just a thought I have occasionally. You'll move along in time.*

4. Take this next moment to follow your breathing, in and out. Each breath holds the doorway to being more present and aware of right here and now.

5. After you have observed and acknowledged your experience, allow your thoughts to flow in and flow out, without reacting. Notice the scary thoughts and let them be. Resist the urge to label them "good" or "bad." You might just say silently: *Come on in if you like—it doesn't matter to me. You're just thoughts. I won't take it personally if you're here.* Let all thoughts announce themselves and be here. There's no need to run away because you see them for what they truly are: thoughts that can't harm you. In fact, many panicky thoughts won't be around once you recover from this difficult moment.

The best way to alleviate intrusive "what if" thinking around your fears of serious illness is to simply allow them their space by not trying to force them to go away. All thoughts and fears eventually follow their own path, coming and going as they please. May you move gently through your day with a peaceful mind.

*

DISSIPATE ALL-CONSUMING THOUGHTS

Have you ever felt stuck in a habitual or repetitive thought or set of thoughts? You might be fixated on something in the past or future. Your mind goes around and around, like a hamster on a treadmill, caged by these all-consuming thoughts. A woman who lives with having panic attacks regularly shared a reoccurring thought that she has: *"If I think about my feelings and how scared I am right now, it will never end. It's dangerous to dwell on my fears because I will always be scared about everything. I try endlessly to stop myself from thinking about my fears, but all I can think about are my endless fears."* It's hard to get off the wheel. You may find yourself spinning through a thought for a few seconds, and then after a few minutes you're recycling the exact same thought as before. Round and round you go again, with no exit strategy in sight.

Since you cannot determine when a panic attack will erupt, let's imagine that you're at home or at work. The following meditation requires being seated. You will want to find a quiet, comfortable place to begin this next meditation. You should be seated upright on a cushion or chair where you can be alert and feel supported. A quiet environment, where you will not be distracted or interrupted, is ideal. Remember to turn off electronic devices that might disturb your meditation.

Take this brief moment to acknowledge and congratulate yourself for taking quality time to meditate and be present.

Begin with paying attention to your breathing. Become aware of the ebb and flow of each breath, in and out. Notice the natural rhythm and pace of your breathing. You may notice the cooler air being retrieved through your mouth and nose, down into the lungs and belly, filling your whole body with life. Next, notice the warmer air being released out through the mouth or nose, leaving the belly, lungs, and throat, loosening your whole body, head to toe.

Gently shift your focus to any physical sensations in your body. Bringing awareness into your body and being mindful of any and all subtle or distinct sensations emanating inside or outside in this unfolding moment. Notice your breathing and how that feels. Notice any itches, aches, stiffness, warmth, dampness, or other sensations. Notice the changing of sensations, coming and going, occurring and disappearing.

Be mindful now of any sounds that arise in your meditation. As you open your awareness to the world of sounds happening around you, listen carefully to the changes in the sounds—a bus roars by and quiets, a refrigerator clinks as it makes more ice and then stops, a phone rings in your neighbor's apartment and then goes quiet. Notice how sounds rise and then fade. Sounds come and go of their own accord, like the waves of an ocean. Everything is moving with the natural flow of life, just like your breathing.

Leaving the sounds behind, take this mindful moment to observe and experience whatever thoughts and feelings come up for you at this time. You may experience chronic and reoccurring worries, such as: I'm really terrified that I won't pass my driver's test. I'm terrible at taking tests because I always freeze and forget everything under pressure. How will I ever get to work again? I have to pass this test, or I won't be able to get to work and then I'll lose my job. I'm scared of taking tests because my mind goes blank. I'll lose everything if I don't pass this test. *You may have experienced similar upsetting and all-consuming thoughts when you are feeling panicked.*

Take this moment now to bear witness to your chronic and never-ending thoughts. Just watching and experiencing your thoughts and feelings like the movement of fish in a stream, passing by, swimming about, and then moving on down with the current. Your thoughts and feelings are just passing schools of fish, here now and then gone again. Notice that no one is actually controlling these panicky thoughts and feelings—they just occur and then vanish. They're just states of mind, flowing along like the stream, carrying a variety of sensations and experiences, memories and repetitious thoughts, always changing and moving. Remember to tune in to your breathing as often as you like, joining with this moment of now.

You may experience times when your mind wants to wander and lose track of your practice. Your mind is very busy and has a tendency to trail off. Suddenly you remember a phone call you need to make or an appointment that you need to double check the time for. When this happens, simply return to your breathing and acknowledge that your mind is wandering right now. The moment you realize that you're not present, you are.

The final step in your meditation is choiceless awareness. Become conscious of whatever thoughts and feelings are predominantly surfacing for you in the present moment. Just watching, witnessing, and experiencing all the passing thoughts, feelings, and sensations. Begin to notice the moment-by-moment changing experience of your mind and body. You are surrounded by the ever-changing nature of life. You are learning to ride the waves of your panic. You will come to learn that your repetitious and panicky thoughts don't last forever and that they gradually fade away. You are becoming aware that your thoughts are just part of the current of life, a passing state of mind and not the whole picture of who you are and what your life is about.

May each breath help you relax and quiet your mind. May each moment greet you with serenity.

*

CALM YOUR FEAR
OF BEING ALONE

Despite technology that allows instant communication over long distances and a growing list of "cyberfriends" through your online social networks, you may still feel terribly alone. When a fear of aloneness triggers feelings of panic, agonizing thoughts might start spinning in your mind like a scratched CD that keeps repeating the same lyrics. You might replay an argument that you had with your partner or friend. Or you might retrace past mistakes, determined to find the cause for why you feel so desperately alone and why no one can help you. Ruminating conjures negative thinking, in a self-perpetuating cycle. You may overthink and obsess about past situations or bad feelings to the point that you're unable to push past the cycle of negative thoughts.

When your panic and fears of being alone hold you hostage with repetitive thoughts, leaving you feeling insecure, anxious, and possibly depressed, steal a few minutes from your day for the following version of "Pause, Observe/Experience, and Allow." No time like the present to get immediate help to slacken the grip of obsessive, negative thoughts.

You can do this practice sitting or standing, as long as you're comfortable and fully alert.

1. Pause by bringing your attention to your breath. On the inhale, be aware of how your breath feels rushing into your body. On the exhale, notice how your breath feels escaping your body. Air in, air out. Follow your breath for about a minute.

2. Observe and experience every little detail of what is coming up in your mind and body. Notice where you might be experiencing tension in your body. Are you holding stress or tightness in your jaw, shoulders, or back? Are you fighting to hold back tears? Notice what emotions are circling in your mind. Are you feeling disconnected, lonely, or unfulfilled? What thoughts are circulating in your brain? Each thought is like a tiny spark zipping about randomly in your brain. Some thoughts keep recirculating, and others vanish.

3. During this practice, you may experience an urge to judge and place a value on your thoughts and feelings. The soundtrack of a judgmental mind might say: *This is bad. That is good. This is fair. That is unfair. This is stupid. That is great.* These judgments can trigger intense emotions while intensifying your panic, making it harder for you to be present. When this happens, simply direct your attention back to your breath and refocus on your thoughts. Notice how thoughts cross your mind like clouds floating in the sky or brief electrical impulses darting around your brain, always moving and disappearing. Allow the judgment to float by.

4. Continue to observe whatever thoughts and feelings arise and allow them to just be what they are, observable parts of your mind and body. Allow all thoughts to drift on by, transient and fleeting, constantly moving, shifting and drifting.

Sit calmly with the weather report of the mind and body, watching the changing cloud formations overhead. If you do this practice regularly, you will experience greater levels of freedom and contentment.

*

FIND FREEDOM FROM THOUGHTS OF DEATH

Rumination on death is common for many people who suffer with panic. You may have watched a close friend or family member die or had a brush with death yourself. When these memories get triggered, you may find yourself thinking obsessively about those who have died, your grief, the loss, and all of the painful experiences from your past. Or you may face your own mortality with accompanying panicky thoughts. A continuous loop of death-related thoughts and fears can make you feel trapped and unable to stop dwelling on death.

Since you can never predict when your rumination and panic will hit, let's imagine a normal, real-life situation, such as sitting down to eat your lunch. As mentioned earlier, the practice of "Pause, Observe/Experience, and Allow" is an important skill to help free you from the plague of ruminating thoughts of any kind and at any time.

1. Take this moment to pause before you eat. You may want to close your eyes and settle more comfortably into your chair. Be aware of your posture, sitting tall and alert.

2. Focus on your breathing. Each breath is a step toward deepening your awareness of the present moment. Breathe in and out from the belly and reflect on what's happening for you in this moment. Pay attention to what you can smell, hear, and feel. Your lunch might be making your mouth water. You might hear car doors open and close on the street. You might feel the warmth emanating from your hot beverage.

3. Go ahead and start eating your lunch, but stay focused on this mindful practice.

4. Observe and experience what's going on with your body sensations, thoughts, and emotions. Your stomach might gently growl. You might feel tense. You might notice your thoughts racing over the same lines: *I can't stop thinking about how my dad died. I miss him all the time. He's never coming back. I will never see him again. I don't think I can go to work today.* Round and round your thoughts may go, many of them repeating over and over again. It's okay. Thoughts have a way of spiraling in the mind. You may notice unrelated thoughts like: *I feel bloated. I can't stand my job. I wonder who just texted me.* Observe each thought and let it be. It's just the natural flow of thoughts.

5. Take this moment to allow your thoughts to be, making room for them to express themselves however they need to. You may experience a strong desire to push away "bad" thoughts and feelings, to repress or stop them. It doesn't feel comfortable to sit with panic-filled thoughts. For this practice, however, allow yourself to simply experience your panic and fears of death, rather than trying to push these things away.

6. You may notice how some thoughts are brief and fleeting, while other thoughts are persistent and keep returning. Notice how thoughts arise and then pass. Observe how old thoughts are replaced by new ones, even unrelated ones, and always changing—for everything is certain to change. That is the one certainty in life. Your thoughts are like

storm clouds that pass overhead, which eventually make way for the sun.

7.   Savor the rest of your meal and enjoy your day!

Make this a part of your informal practice of mindfulness that you can carry with you into any activity, whenever your panic and ruminating thoughts take over your normal routine. As you notice how transient your thoughts are, you will become less reactive to and less trapped by them.

*

QUIET YOUR FEARS
OF THE UNKNOWN

Many people fear not knowing what might happen if there is not enough information to make a reasonable prediction. For example, some people fear being in a lake or ocean because they cannot see the bottom or what is under them or what might be near them. Others have a fear of the dark. If you are experiencing panic around your fear of the unknown or a fear of not knowing what to expect in your present situation, then you might be all too familiar with the kind of habitual thought patterns that can hijack your mind. These thoughts are frequently chronic, negative, and ingrained, and they may sound like this: *I can't do that because something awful will happen to me. I can't try anything new because I might get in trouble. I don't want to go someplace that I've never been because I won't know what to expect.*

When your fear of the unknown feels suffocating and you feel plagued by chronic worry and fearful thoughts, try this mindful sitting meditation to help expand your understanding of panicky thoughts and loosen their stranglehold on you. Sitting meditation, as you may recall from earlier in the chapter, is designed to bring awareness to five meditative components: the breath, physical sensations, sounds, mind states, and choiceless awareness. Let's explore each of those in depth now.

Find a safe, quiet, and comfortable place to sit in a chair or on a cushion, keeping fully alert and wakeful. Be sure to turn off any electronic devices that might interrupt or disturb your meditation. Feel free to set an alarm, if your time for meditation is limited.

Your practice commences when you become mindful of your breathing. Each breath is your personal guide into the present moment. With each in and out breath, acknowledge your fear of the unknown. Take several breaths now, and pay attention to how each breath feels in your body.

Now, gradually shift your mindful attention to whatever physical sensations ensue. Bring awareness into your whole body and notice any distinct or demanding sensations that you're experiencing. You may experience a painful stiffening of muscles in your neck and shoulders, or waves of nausea in your stomach. While staying connected to your breathing, air flowing in and air flowing out, notice the ever-changing nature of your sensations. You may notice a pain in one area, then it moves into another area. You may feel the urge to sneeze, and then it passes. You may feel tingles, aches, stiffness, or your pulse, followed by so many variations of sensations, appearing and disappearing. Sensations continuously emerge and go away.

On your mindful journey, you will now extend your awareness to sounds and what you can hear at this time. Listen closely to any subtle or harsh sounds in your vicinity or beyond. As with the sensations, you may notice how sounds come and go, rise and then vanish, with the organic flow of nature and change. Sounds arise of their own accord and leave on their own. They appear to be ownerless, simply sounds that come and go.

Leaving behind the focus on sounds, contemplate the mind states with regard to your thoughts and feelings as the focus of your meditation. A variety of thoughts may come to your mind: I feel scared about tomorrow's work meeting because I don't know what to expect. Why does my mother always call when I'm the most stressed out? I can't remember the last time I watered my plants. *Begin to direct your awareness to the thought process itself.*

Simply witness and experience your mind without clinging to or resisting any thoughts or emotions that come up. Let yourself acknowledge the myriad of fluctuating mental processes or formations in this ever-evolving moment of now.

Perhaps it might be like lying in a chaise lounge outside, on a warm evening, watching the stars and constellations tracing the night sky. You might experience the mind in the same way. Stars, like thoughts, come into focus, some brighter, some weaker, and then pass overhead. These are just states of mind, changing with the course of time and moving along their natural path. You are cultivating mindfulness when you detach from the storyline of your thoughts and just experience the external thought as a thought—a thought generated from the mind, vocal at times, quiet at other times, just thoughts without an owner or driver.

Remember to stay tuned in to your breathing. Each breath is a window into the present moment. This moment right now.

Through choiceless awareness, you are allowing whatever might be happening for you in this breath, sensation, sound, or state of mind. Feel into your body and observe the ever-changing starry sky like the ever-changing thoughts and feelings of your mind and body. At one moment, your attention may be drawn to something acute and panicky. The next moment, your chin itches and your panic diminishes. Everything is constantly changing—your mood and the stars, your thoughts and the seasons, your worries and the weather. It's just the nature of things to be continually shifting. Observe and let them be.

As you gently shift away from choiceless awareness, return to the breath and feel your entire mind and body connected to this orchestra of experiences. May you feel peace and tranquility greeting you at every step and wherever you go.

*

FEEL COMFORTABLE AROUND OTHERS

For most of us, there is no way to completely avoid people in life. If you have acute anxiety, panic, or discomfort in the presence of other people, then you may avoid social events or being in public at all costs. You may experience severe shyness or lack of self-confidence when meeting people or making introductions. You may also not like to be the center of attention. Since you can rarely avoid people and gatherings, you may often feel as if another panic attack is waiting just around the corner.

The following applied practice will guide you step by step and moment by moment through "Pause, Observe/Experience, and Allow," to help you harness your innate ability to find balance and ease in every panicky moment.

You can do this anywhere, whether seated or standing.

1. Take a thoughtful pause to congratulate yourself for committing to this practice right now. This conscious decision to bring mindfulness into your mind and body is important to your overall well-being and peace of mind.

2. Pay attention to your breathing—the rhythm and cycle, the rising and falling, and the sound of air passing into and out of your nose and mouth and body. Be with your breath, pause, and be present.

3. Make space for noticing any thoughts that may be generated at this time. Be aware of any emotions, thoughts, and sensations that present themselves. You might find yourself saying: *Oh look, there's that worry about the upcoming*

conference that I have to attend. Look again, there's that nagging fear about the lunch date with my friend at the outdoor restaurant. Here comes that reoccurring and uncomfortable thought about everyone looking at me. More thoughts arrive, like uninvited guests, and more thoughts depart, without so much as a good-bye. Notice how they come and they go at their leisure. Nothing stays the same. No thought, feeling, or sensation is ever fixed and permanent.

4. Simply allow whatever comes to mind to be. Remember that whatever arises passes away. When you don't fight it, when you just let your thoughts be the way they are, you will begin to notice how impermanent your panicky thoughts can be, and the mind can steady itself with this acknowledgment. You are learning to let things be and learning to go with the flow of your changing mental landscape.

5. Return to your breathing and reconnect with the unfolding moment that is right here before you.

May you embrace the beauty of change. May you find ease of mind.

*

Here We Are

As we come to the end of this chapter, you have been introduced to sitting meditation and the "Pause, Observe/Experience, and Allow" practice for dealing with the rush of panic in your thoughts. You also carried out and reflected on some mindful practices that you can bring into your daily activities to help you deal with panic. We recommend that you continue to use the meditations, mindfulness in daily activities, and S.T.O.P. and R.A.I.N. every day.

The next chapter is our last, and we want to send you off with hope and encouragement that you can live a life beyond panic. You will be introduced to loving-kindness meditation and the "web of life" meditation, along with some informal mindful practices to grow a sense of interconnection with the web of life.

chapter 4

Life Beyond Panic

Before picking up this book, you may have never imagined that you could live a life with less panic. We hope that by now you are already doing so, or at least have a glimpse of what's possible. Thus far you've explored and learned practices of working with panic in the body, in your emotions, and in your thoughts. In this last chapter we want to explore with you how to connect to the richness of life beyond the immediate physical, emotional, and mental experiences of panic.

We trust that you now understand that this journey is an opportunity for greater self-discovery and a gateway into your heart for deeper wisdom and compassion. As you work with panic and learn from it, you will cultivate greater understanding of yourself and the world around you, and this will make you feel more alive, connected, and free. You'll come to know that you're part of this great universe and can feel more at home within it. This is what we mean when we speak about a life beyond panic.

Albert Einstein, who was known for his wisdom as well as his scientific genius, points to the interconnectedness of existence in an excerpt from one of his letters, published in the *New York Post* (November 28, 1972):

> A human being is part of the whole, called by us the Universe, a part limited in time and space. He experiences himself, his thoughts and feelings, as something separate from the rest—a kind of optical delusion of his consciousness. This delusion is a kind of prison for us, restricting us to our personal desires and to affection for a few persons nearest to us. Our task must be to free ourselves from this prison by widening our circle of compassion to embrace all living creatures and the whole of nature in its beauty.

To help dissolve this illusion of separateness, we would like to introduce you to the formal MBSR practice of loving-kindness meditation as well as the "web of life" meditation for cultivating feelings of safety, compassion, and love. Over time, these practices will increase your feelings of connection not only to yourself, but also to your family, friends, work associates, and fellow living beings, the world around you, and the universe.

It's also fair to say that most of us have already tasted or had glimpses of this interconnectedness to the "web of life" but may have not fully recognized that it was happening because we were so absorbed in the experience itself. Here are some examples: a time you spent watching a beautiful sunrise or sunset, or out on a beautiful walk in nature, or having an intimate moment with someone you love that made you feel so connected that everything felt just perfect. In such moments, most likely all your panic was gone and you had a sense that you were part of a big and beautiful universe and that everything was not just okay, but exquisite. We trust that you've had brief moments like these, and through mindfulness, loving-kindness, and "web of life" practices you'll experience more of them.

Loving-Kindness Meditation

Loving-kindness meditation is a very powerful practice for moving your heart to greater compassion and love for yourself, all living beings, and the world. When your heart is open and not closed or hardened with panic, you can journey through life with greater ease of being. Just as lighting a small candle can dispel the darkness, a heart filled with loving-kindness dispels the panic all around it.

It's also important to mention that sometimes when you practice loving-kindness meditation, it can bring up feelings opposite to loving-kindness, such as resentment, anger, envy, sadness, and even rage. We want you to know that this is normal and that there's actually a reason why these opposite feelings arise. They are showing you directly and clearly where you're stuck or holding back from loving-kindness. Therefore it's important to identify and acknowledge any unresolved feelings and work to reconcile them. This act of making amends will begin to open the doorway and heal your heart. As you acknowledge your emotional pain, your compassion and love will naturally grow and flow. By bringing mindfulness to whatever you're feeling, you'll gradually find your way into your heart and the hearts of others. May you hold yourself with great care, compassion, and kindness.

FOUNDATIONAL PRACTICE:
Loving-Kindness Meditation

As in other formal meditations, find a quiet place and sit upright on a cushion or chair. If you prefer, you may lie down on a bed or carpet, as long as you can remain alert and comfortable. Turn off your phone and any other electronic device that could disturb you. Read and practice the script for this guided meditation below, pausing briefly after each paragraph, or feel free to download a recording from New Harbinger Publications at newharbinger.com/25264. You can download a fifteen-, thirty-, or forty-five-minute version.

As you practice this meditation, if any of the phrases in the script do not resonate with you, feel free to replace them with ones that do. Once you learn the spirit of loving-kindness meditation, you can make it your own. Let it be alive and real and not just some formulaic recitation of words or phrases that have little meaning and vitality to you.

Begin your practice by congratulating yourself that you are dedicating some precious time for meditation.

As you begin to stop and become present, bring your awareness to your body and mind and check in with yourself on how you're feeling physically, mentally, and emotionally, and acknowledge whatever is present. This might be the first time you are stopping today, so just feel what is present within you without any censorship. Simply allowing and acknowledging whatever is within and just letting it be without evaluation, judgment, or any form of analysis.

Gradually, shift the focus of your awareness to the breath, breathing normally and naturally. As you breathe in, be aware of breathing in, and as you breathe out, be aware of breathing out. Just being aware of breathing.

You are welcome to focus your breathing on the abdomen or nose, depending on your preference. Just living life one inhalation and one exhalation at a time, breathing in and breathing out.

Now gently bring your awareness into your heart area, feeling any waves of sensations and allowing them to go wherever they need to go.

The heart is the gateway into deeper compassion and love for yourself and for all beings. Feel into your own precious heart and life with compassion, mercy, and love. Know that you are doing the best you can and that all of your past has led you into this moment that can now be met with greater understanding and compassion.

Feel into the powerful qualities of loving-kindness itself, a boundless love that can be compared to the moon, stars, or sun, all of which shine on all living beings without separation, distinction, or prejudice.

Bring this love into your own heart and feel it absorb into all the cells of your body and your being. May you open to deep kindness and compassion for yourself just as you are, imperfectly perfect as you are.

At times you may struggle to feel loving or compassionate toward yourself. If so, work with this by acknowledging your feelings, whatever they are.

It may be helpful at times to reflect upon the following phrases, letting them sink into your being. If you find the phrases helpful, use them; if you find them not helpful or difficult to relate to, make up your own. May you trust your inner knowing to find the gateway into your heart.

May I be safe.
May I be healthy.

May I have ease of body and mind.
May I be at peace.

Now expand the field of loving-kindness to your teachers, mentors, and others who have inspired you, repeating the same phrases:

May my teachers and my mentors be safe.
May my teachers and my mentors be healthy.
May my teachers and my mentors have ease of body and mind.
May my teachers and my mentors be at peace.

Now gradually expand the field of loving-kindness to those near and dear to you, such as your family, friends, and community:

May my near and dear ones be safe.
May my near and dear ones be healthy.
May my near and dear ones have ease of body and mind.
May my near and dear ones be at peace.

Now further extend the field of loving-kindness to people you feel neutral toward, such as acquaintances and strangers:

May my neutral ones be safe.
May my neutral ones be healthy.
May my neutral ones have ease of body and mind.
May my neutral ones be at peace.

Now consider extending loving-kindness to those who give you difficulty, such as your enemies. It may seem challenging or even next to impossible to send loving-kindness to this group, so it may be wise to first consider whether you get any benefit from holding grudges. Does holding a grudge promote your health and well-being? For many people it does not, and you may begin to understand that at the very least it is more skillful to work on neutralizing these strong feelings that can be so toxic to your being.

You can begin by sending compassion to yourself and then wisely reflecting upon reconciliation and considering that reconciliation is really for your benefit and not the other person's. You may even begin to see more clearly that the causes of people's hurting one another are fear and unawareness and that perhaps neither you nor the difficult person is "bad," merely unaware and scared.

May you open your heart and extend loving-kindness even to the difficult ones, and then further extend the wish that they each find the gateway into their own hearts, gaining greater awareness and transforming their fear into love. Gently and slowly send loving-kindness to your difficult ones or enemies:

> May my difficult ones be safe.
> May my difficult ones be healthy.
> May my difficult ones have ease of body and mind.
> May my difficult ones be at peace.

Now taking some time to remember those who are going through hard times, both those you know personally and those you don't, and extending your goodwill and wishes of healing. Letting none be forsaken, may those who are suffering in any way be at peace.

Building this loving-kindness energy to become as boundless as the sky and beginning to radiate it to all human beings and all living beings. Sending loving-kindness to all living beings near and far, even those yet to be born. May all beings be at ease.

Sending this vast love to all beings who live on or in the earth, in the water, and in the air, spreading loving-kindness in all directions:

May all beings be safe.
May all beings be healthy.
May all beings have ease of body and mind.
May all beings be at peace.

Now extend this love outward, without boundaries or limits, into the solar system and then throughout the universe.

May all beings everywhere be safe, be healthy, and dwell with peace.

Gently now returning to the breath, feeling your whole body, as you breathe in and out. Feel the entire body rising on an inhalation and falling on an exhalation. Feeling the body as a complete organism that is connected and whole. Feel how you are connected to the earth below you and to all that is around and above you. Feeling yourself to be a precious part of this "web of life," interconnected to it all.

As you come to the end of this meditation, take a moment to congratulate yourself for the time you have spent, and may you share any merits you have gained with all beings. Begin to gently wiggle your toes and fingers, opening your eyes and being here and now.

May all beings be at peace.

*

How to Practice Loving-Kindness Meditation

We recommend that you incorporate loving-kindness meditation into your formal practice of mindfulness by following any other meditation, such as mindful breathing, the body scan, or sitting meditation, with a short, abbreviated loving-kindness meditation. This will really help balance your practice of mindfulness and decrease moments of panic as you open to more safety and compassion for yourself. You are also welcome to practice loving-kindness meditation solely whenever you like. Some people prefer a daily practice, while others practice it once a week or as desired. Find a time that works best for you, since everyone is different. Whatever time you do it is the best time. Let this be a practice you look forward to doing, a gift to yourself as a way to become more balanced within your body and mind. Feel free to use an alarm clock or timer.

The Web of Life

We would like to now introduce you to the "web of life" practice, a simple and yet profound reminder of the sacredness and interconnectedness of life. You can do this practice anywhere, at any time, to help decrease panic and transform your life.

Take a moment right now to open to your senses. Look around the room and notice colors and shapes. Listen to sounds, smell any scents, bring your awareness to any tastes lingering in your mouth, and feel any sensations in your body and let them all be. Just be present with all that's here in this moment, without trying to change anything. Acknowledge any thoughts and emotions you're feeling, and let them be as well. As you let things be, feel your place in this universe; you are neither more nor less than anyone else. The very elements that make up your body are made from the universe, and you can never be separated from it.

Life is indeed made of moments. See whether you can pause and reflect on how we are all so integrally connected to one another—we all breathe and share the same air and live in this world. As you experience more deeply this interconnected "web of life," your panic will gradually fade away. You will begin to feel safe and at ease, knowing that you have not been forsaken, and you will find that you are living a life beyond panic.

FOUNDATIONAL PRACTICE:
The "Web of Life" Meditation

Find a comfortable position on a cushion or chair or lying on a bed or the floor. Turn off your phone or other devices so you can remain undisturbed. Read and practice the script for this guided meditation below, pausing briefly after each paragraph, or feel free to download a recording from New Harbinger Publications at newharbinger.com/25264.

Begin by taking a few moments to arrive and settle in by bringing your awareness into your mind and body. Acknowledge how you are feeling and let it be.

Gently shift to mindful breathing, being aware of breathing in and out...no need to manipulate the breath in any way—just breathing in and out, normally and naturally.

Now begin to feel the connection of your body on the chair, cushion, bed, or mat, and feel its connection to the floor. Reflect on the connection of the floor to the building you are in and its connection to the earth farther below.

Feel that sense of being held by the earth below you, and just allow yourself to be held by the earth. You are in a safe space, and you can breathe in and out with ease in your body and mind.

Feel how the earth rises up to hold and embrace you. There is nothing more you need to do, nowhere you have to go, and no one you have to be. Just being held in the heart of kindness and letting be.

Reflect on your loved ones being held in the same way—with safety and ease of body and mind. Reflect on how the earth holds all beings, whether they are acquaintances, strangers, or difficult ones—with no bias, no discrimination, no separation.

Reflect on how this earth holds all beings, forsaking none— whether they be small or large.

Reflect on how this earth does not exist in a vacuum, that it is connected to a solar system and vast universe. We all are interconnected. Our bodies and the earth, the sun and the stars, are composed of the same matter—the same basic particles, joined in different ways.

Feeling into that sense of connection and interconnection that we are all made of stardust. Feeling that sense of being home within your body and mind with a true sense of belonging and connection.

Just breathing in and out, feeling the grace of this universe—no isolation nor separation, feeling that sense of connection and interconnection and being at home in your being. Nothing more you need to do, go, get, or push away. Imperfectly perfect as you are, resting in the heart of this universe.

May all beings here and everywhere dwell with peace.

*

How to Practice The "Web of Life" Meditation

You are welcome to practice this meditation any time that it feels useful for you. Make it your own and let it begin to seep into your life. You can be creative with this practice, like Eli in the story below. As you practice the "web of life," you will feel more connected to yourself and all of life.

* Eli's Story

Eli had lived with panic for a long time. Even in childhood, he was jumpy and startled easily. He couldn't quite identify where this all came from, but when he was in college he realized that he needed to do something about it because the panic was deeply affecting his life.

Eli heard about mindfulness and decided to learn more. As he brought more awareness into himself, he could see that he wasn't feeling so secure with the world and the universe. The world felt really big, so big that at times he felt out of control and feared that he would lose himself, like being swallowed and consumed.

Eli learned how to do the loving-kindness and "web of life" meditations—he especially liked the sense of interconnection at the end of these meditations, which made him feel safe. One day while he was sitting in a park near his home, he decided to try the "web of life" practice that he had learned, and he made it his own. He began by being mindful of his breathing and then reflected on how the oxygen he was receiving was being offered to him by the plant life and trees around him, and that the carbon dioxide he exhaled, in turn, fed the plants and trees around him. As he reflected on how he and the plant world reciprocated each other in perfect harmony and union, he felt wonderful. Quite spontaneously a feeling of the interconnectedness of life—how we all support one another to live in this world and universe—washed over him.

Eli began to take time during his day to notice and experience this interconnection to the "web of life." When he was in the gym, he would watch people working out near him, and it seemed as if everyone were dancing together. People were moving in unison, a collage of shapes and sizes exercising together in harmony, with a common humanity. He began to see these interconnections just about everywhere he went: at the bank, at the store, at home, and at work. There were times when Eli would go to the edge of the ocean, look out over the grand expanse of the mingling of the sea and sky, and breathe in and out and feel his connection to himself, the world, and the universe. Eli found his true home and felt safe in the midst of it all.

Applied Practices

Let's move now into some applied practices to cultivate a sense of ease and peace beyond panic.

CONTENTMENT

Have you ever noticed that a great deal of your day is spent waiting? Most likely you wait to pump your gas, you wait to purchase items, you wait to speak to someone in person, you wait for access to the photocopier or fax machine, and you wait on the phone to be helped. The rush of panic may find you at any one of these times. If you're experiencing a panic attack, perhaps while waiting in a dreaded line, this next mindful breathing practice will help nurture feelings of abundance and thriving.

You can do mindful breathing in any position—sitting, standing, or even while moving—so long as you are at ease and attentive.

1. To connect fully with the present moment, you need to pay deep and nonjudgmental attention. Start with the breath. Breathe mindfully for about a minute. Become a kind observer of your own breath sensations as the air moves in and out of your body. As you become a more sensitive observer, notice different qualities in each breath, in or out, and the space and stillness between the breaths as well. Bring your attention to the physical sensations of your breathing. Focus on one part of your body, such as your nose or abdomen, where you can actually feel your breath moving in and out. Allow your attention to rest there. Air rushing in. Air rushing out.

2. You may notice at times that your mind will want to wander. Inattentiveness, distraction, and mindlessness are common and frequent obstacles to staying in the present moment. Not paying attention to what you are doing can separate

you from the richness in every moment of life. When you notice that your mind is elsewhere, simply pay attention on purpose to your breathing and you will easily return to being present. You've done nothing wrong. The mind likes to wander and will do it countless times. Each time, gently but firmly bring your attention back.

3. With your next breath, set your intentions for this practice, stating what you would like to gain by it. On the inhale, say aloud or to yourself: *May this practice connect me with life as it is, with greater contentment. May this practice deepen my awareness to the fullness of each moment.* When you set your intentions, you are sowing the seeds for contentment to take root and grow inside you. You begin to open your gratitude to the wealth of air, beauty, sky, and earth that is supporting you at all times. Feel free to make up your own intentions that resonate more fully with your current situation.

4. As you continue to turn your gentle attention to your breathing, remember to just let each breath be. There's no need to make anything happen or alter anything about yourself. Allow yourself to just be who you are in this moment. You are tracking the patterns of every sensation and breath. Breathe in, pause, breathe out, pause, and so on. Notice the unique character of each breath.

5. End your meditation by shifting your focus off of your breathing and sensations and moving gently into your next activity.

*

SELF-LOVE AND APPRECIATION

No matter how you get it—at home, at the gym, cycling, swimming, running—exercise is an important part of nurturing self-love. Your body is a powerful and marvelous wonder of bones, muscles, blood, and skin. You can move and stretch, lift and turn, twist and fold, and clench and relax. When you think about all the physical limitations that many people confront every day, your body is truly miraculous! Your body is also a perfect subject on which to exercise purposeful awareness, particularly when you're in the throes of a panic attack. This next practice, a version of S.T.O.P., will enhance your appreciation and love for yourself and your body. Try it now.

You can do this practice sitting, standing, lying down, or moving. Make sure that you're in a comfortable position, yet one that supports wakefulness.

1. Begin by tuning into your breath. Each breath holds the key to being alive. Take a minute or two to pay kind attention to your every inhalation and exhalation. Notice all the physical sensations that accompany each breath, and notice where you feel your breath in your body.

2. Observe whatever you're thinking, feeling, or sensing in your mind and body in this moment. A vast array of messages will pour out of you, such as *I'm thirsty. My foot hurts. I feel exhausted. I wish my boyfriend would call. When will I feel better?* Acknowledge any and all emotions and sensations that come up, and allow them to follow their own course. Notice how you have a degree of control over some thoughts but not others. Some feelings are prominent and

want your attention. Some sensations are subtle and then evaporate. All the things that you experience in your mind and body are like passengers in a moving train, with each passenger representing different mental, emotional, and physical parts of yourself. For example, one passenger is your negative self-talk, another passenger is your worry, and yet another passenger is your fatigue.

3. Remember to tune in to your breathing and resume being present.

4. Take this conscious moment to practice beginner's mind. If you skip over all the little experiences, you may slide back into mindlessness. So keep looking to see something new, as if you are a child noticing how your body works for the first time. You can learn something new even if it is something you have already explored a hundred times before. With practice, beginner's mind will help you develop a sense of awe, a feeling of excitement and wonder in your practice of mindfulness.

5. Now, if you have been moving, stop and return to a stationary position, such as sitting, standing, or lying down. Take this moment to experience some stillness in your body. Lean into the stillness by following your heartbeat or your breath. Notice where stillness lives in your body—perhaps your belly or face or feet. Feel this peaceful stillness radiate throughout every part of your body—your limbs, torso, fingers, toes, ears, and mouth. Remember, you carry this stillness within you at all times. When you befriend this reservoir of stillness inside, you'll also find a deeper appreciation for your body.

6. Carry on with your day, practicing kindness and caring for yourself.

Whether you practice gentle movement, such as yoga, tai chi, or qigong, or more rigorous workouts, exercise is an essential part of cultivating a healthy relationship with your body. A mindful awareness of your body during any activity will help you deepen your love for your body and appreciate all that you ask of it and all that it gives to you each day.

*

THE GIFT OF PANIC

No one in their right mind considers panic a blessing. *How can my most agonizing fear produce something beneficial or positive?* You may berate yourself for your panic attacks. You may drive your family nuts with your constant hypervigilance and chronic anxious thoughts and feelings. Your friends may not be able to understand or help you. Your panic may have negatively affected your romantic relationships, career, and vacations over the years. And no pill has ever cured panic attacks.

You may ask, *Just how could anything positive possibly come out of being riddled with sudden and extremely intense episodes of palpations, uncontrollable shaking, light-headedness, and hot flushes, combined with racing emotions and thoughts of worst-case scenarios and fears?* "Show me the gift of panic when all I can see is a long list of negatives," you may demand.

This next practice will help you highlight the pearls of wisdom that often get overlooked at the peak of your panic. You can do it at home or at work. May it be a useful reminder during a panic attack for planting the seeds of what your panicky thoughts and feelings are here to teach you and the hidden blessing behind the panic.

Seated comfortably or lying down, check in with your posture and begin when you are feeling attentive and awake.

1. Breathe mindfully for several breaths to remain steady and present for the unfolding experience of now. Let yourself soften and open to noticing every small aspect of each breath: the in, the out, the rise, the fall, of each inhale and exhale.

2. Set your intentions for this practice. Speak kindly, quietly, and reassuringly to the hurt part of yourself that carries the heavy burden of your panic-ridden life:

May I embrace my panic as a gift so that it will reveal to me what is fueling these panicky feelings. May I embrace my panic so that it will give me deeper insight and wisdom into the panic and set me free.

May I embrace my panic as a gift that is teaching me to be more compassionate and empathetic to others and myself.

May I embrace my panic as a gift that I have harnessed and redirected into creative outlets, such as arts and crafts, gardening, exercise, or _____ (fill in the blank).

May I embrace my panic as a gift that allows me to be rich with a vast array of feelings and emotions.

May I embrace my panic as a gift that has taught me to be a wise, careful, and cautious parent, caretaker, teacher, business-person, or _____ (fill in the blank).

May I embrace my panic as a gift that gives me a deeper appreciation and understanding of the complexity of life.

May I embrace my panic as a gift that _____ (fill in the blank).

3. Slowly follow your breath and congratulate yourself for taking this time to acknowledge a few of the positive things that panic has taught you.

When the voice of criticism starts putting you down, take a mindful moment to reflect on the positive lessons that you've taken with you from your experience of panic. Feel free to write these blessings on a piece of paper and hang it on your fridge or desk, as loving reminders that panic is more than it seems. Panic can be your teacher, a guide that can lead you to learn more about your strengths and beauty within.

*

BALANCE AND JOY

It can be challenging to bring mindfulness into your busy workday. If you do get a few minutes to yourself, you may have only enough time to grab a bite to eat before you're rushing back to the next pressing deadline or commitment. Perhaps this is all the more reason to consider incorporating a few mindful minutes of a self-inquiry R.A.I.N. practice into your daily grind in order to harvest the fruits of balance and joy. This next mindful moment will bring you closer to what you value most in life, to what really matters to you beyond your panic.

1. Start by bringing your full attention to your breath. Each breath is a bridge that links you to the present moment. Be with each breath, following your breathing pattern as you inhale and exhale, without trying to change or alter it in any way. Let each breath unfold, and notice the physical manifestations of your breathing in your body. Do this for at least three to five breaths.

2. Stay with your breath and begin to *recognize* when a strong thought or feeling occurs. Notice what comes up when you focus on your mind and body.

3. Take this moment to *allow and acknowledge* the mental and emotional storm that is occurring. You can't always ascertain what caused your panic or why you feel what you feel, but you can recognize and acknowledge the symptoms. You might feel light-headed, you might feel a trembling in your body, and you might even feel dizzy. You might feel frightened, anxious, and overwhelmed. This is what panic feels like at times. It's okay. Panic happens.

4. *Investigate,* with detachment and clarity, just the facts. How are these thoughts and feelings affecting your mind and body in this moment? Become a detective and observe how thoughts appear and disappear, how feelings are critical one moment and almost unnoticeable the next. Maybe you feel acute discomfort in one part of your body, then it fades.

5. Take this next moment to bring to mind what you value most in your life. It could be your family, friendship, work, good health, good grades, happiness, safety, love, laughter, or helping others. What are your core values? Pause to reflect on your mental list of what you value. What thoughts and feelings come up when you consider what is most important to you? You may notice that what you value most connects you more intimately with what gives you pleasure or feeds your soul or gives your life more meaning and purpose. What you value ties in directly with your joy, and more joy helps balance you when you feel out of balance due to panicky thoughts. Joy and balance are within you each time you return to your highest values.

6. The final step is *non-identifying,* or not taking your thoughts and feelings personally. For example, when you call a friend and he announces, "I can't talk. I'm heading into a conference with my boss. Sorry, need to run," you know that your friend would talk if he could, and it's not that he doesn't want to talk to you—so you don't take it personally. With non-identifying, you're essentially saying to yourself: *Panic is being experienced. That's all it is. I don't need to fix it or repress it or change myself. It has little to do with me.* As you practice non-identifying, you will begin to challenge the very

foundation of panic. You will open yourself to the possibility of deeper understanding and acceptance.

7. Maybe the old way of pushing panic away isn't the healthiest or most reliable way of coping. By introducing mindful awareness into your core values, you will discover another way of living, beyond your panic and experiencing greater joy and balance in your everyday life.

*

COMPASSION

Can you think back on a time that you shared an intimate moment with someone you love? It could be the last time you sang a lullaby for your child to fall asleep in your arms. It might be the last time you made love to your partner or spouse. Or maybe it was a heart-expansive talk with an old friend whom you cherish and trust. When you hold that loving memory in your mind, how does it make you feel? We bet you feel loved, appreciated, and bursting with compassion and empathy. If only the feeling of open-heartedness would last, you might lament. Well, it can. The following practice, a version of loving-kindness meditation, is remarkable for strengthening feelings of kindness and compassion by actively wishing yourself and others happiness or well-being.

This particular meditation is based on specific phrases of well-wishing; these are provided for you, but feel free to select your own phrases that resonate warmly with your heart. If you've picked up this book in the middle of a panic attack, you may be riding the waves of a raging heartbeat, obsessive thoughts, and feelings of dread. This meditation will also help you transform and find healing in many panicky situations.

1. Find a comfortable seated position—or lie down, if you prefer, as long as you can stay awake and attentive. Bring your attention to your breath, and breathe mindfully for a minute or two.

2. Focus on the emotions in your heart. Notice any feelings or sensations that you are having in your heart space. Let them flow freely, kindly accepting whatever issues forth.

3. You may notice that you do not feel loving or happy or content, especially at first. That is okay. If you feel sad, angry, or resentful, this is perfectly normal and acceptable. These opposite feelings likely reflect times when your painful feelings were repressed—forced into hiding—and you held back from loving-kindness. Simply let the feelings be, gently accepting whatever is released.

4. Allow yourself to open to the good as well, and accept any emotions or thoughts of kindness and open-heartedness. If necessary, you may recollect a warm embrace with someone you care about, or a love note or e-mail, or the love expressed in the eyes of your child. Let the kind remembrances of sensations and feelings wash over you, filling you with as much love and support as possible.

5. Shift your focus to yourself. You will be speaking directly to the part of yourself that is anxious, fearful, or injured or otherwise needs special attention right now. Remember to speak with kindness and compassion, wishing wellness for yourself. Use the following phrases or make up your own:

    May I be safe.

    May I be happy.

    May I be healthy and well.

    May I live with peace and ease in my mind and body.

6. Return to your breath. With each inhale, a radiant, soothing light of loving-kindness is filling your entire being. With each exhale, you may now extend your vibrant light of loving-kindness to one or more people who have helped

guide you in generous and loving ways. Keep this person or these people in mind as you repeat the phrases:

May you be safe.

May you be happy.

May you be healthy and well.

May you live with peace and ease in your mind and body.

7. Again, return to your breath and connect with this present moment. With each breath, in and out, you now gradually expand your light of loving-kindness to others who also struggle with panic. You don't need to know these people personally or even know their names; just extend compassion to all the people right now who live with panic on a daily basis. You are simply wishing others, far and wide, the same relief and ease that you wish for yourself. Breathe mindfully for a few breaths and repeat the phrases below.

May all those who suffer with panic be safe.

May all those who suffer with panic be happy.

May all those who suffer with panic be healthy and well.

May all those who suffer with panic live with peace and ease in their mind and body.

8. Remember to greet with compassion and nonjudgment whatever comes forward inside you. May loving-kindness burn brightly in your heart, shedding its comforting light on everyone in your life and the world.

*

SACREDNESS

Nature provides an excellent backdrop for a "web of life" meditation using all of your senses, and it can offer access to your innate healing and transformative powers to reduce any panicky thoughts, feelings, and sensations that you might be experiencing at the time. This next practice is also a reminder of the sacredness of all life.

If you can head out to the woods or countryside or the ocean for this meditation, do so. You can also imagine that you're out at one of your favorite spots in nature and conjure the things that you love and remember about that place. Otherwise, your backyard, a park, or somewhere with a view of nature will work.

You are welcome to sit, stand, or lie down, maintaining alertness and awareness of your mind and body.

1. Take a few mindful belly breaths and then follow the natural progression of your breathing—the pattern and rhythm of each inhale and each exhale.

2. Open to your sense of sight. Pay attention to every little detail you see around you. Notice gradations of color and variations in shapes. Notice textures and surfaces—the ridges on the tree trunks, the rays of sunlight peering through the branches, the leaves gathered in piles, the clumps of dirt beneath your shoes. Tap into your peripheral vision to the left and right and focus on one particular object. What are you noticing now? Remember to breathe and simply watch.

3. You may experience some doubt about this practice, like a little voice that tells you, *Forget this practice—it won't be able to help you with your panic.* Simply allow this thought to be. Recognize the doubt, acknowledge it, welcome it into your meditation, and then let it be. There's no need to push doubt away or resist it. Your doubt is just a friend traveling in the other direction whom you pass on the trail.

4. Shift your focus to sounds. Take this moment to pay attention to everything you can hear. Simply observe the coming and going of sounds. You may hear the sound of a lawn mower or a rush of water from a creek. In many ways there is little difference between these sounds. All sound is just an auditory phenomenon, or things you can hear. Only your mind attaches value to distinguish between good and bad sounds. Remember to breathe mindfully and listen.

5. Take this next moment to pay attention to your sense of touch. What do you notice immediately that you can feel with your body? You may notice that your hands feel warm but your face is cool from a breeze. You may notice any pain or tension stored up in your body. This is just your body asking you to pay attention to it. What do you feel just beneath your fingertips? Breathe mindfully and feel.

6. Begin to awaken to your sense of taste. Draw attention to your mouth, tongue, and saliva. Did you have a coffee or tea today? Is the essence of your last meal still present in your mouth? Breathe mindfully and acknowledge what you taste in this moment.

7. Leaving taste behind, gently shift your focus to your sense of smell. What aromas stand out to you? You may notice smells that you find unpleasant or uncomfortable, such as car exhaust or body odor. Simply acknowledge the smell and allow it to be, neither good nor bad. Smells are just smells. Breathe mindfully and allow any tension or panicky sensations in your body to drop to the earth.

8. Check in with your emotions. How did this exploration of your senses make you feel? You may feel more grounded and connected. You may notice a great many more details about your surroundings. Feel the earth lovingly cradling you and all of your fears in her arms without any judgment. You may notice a newfound relationship with the earth—from the ground that you walk on to the water that you drink to the air that you breathe, all of which support and sustain life—based on wholehearted and unconditional acceptance. This is the sacredness built into the "web of life." What feels sacred to you right now?

Mindful recognition of each of your senses also connects you directly with the world around you. Through sensory meditation, you allow for time to be still in nature, which in turn creates a stillness of mind. May you carry this peaceful stillness and awareness of all that is sacred with you at all times.

*

HAPPINESS AND LOVE

If you're a busy bee and a multitasker, you may find that even on your days off, you just don't get the rest and relaxation that your mind and body need and crave. When you're at home doing endless chores—watering the plants, emptying the trash, sweeping the floor—the following practice will assist you in deepening your connection to what you value most in life, such as happiness and love.

If you're currently dealing with panicky thoughts or feelings, give yourself permission to take a restful moment to pause, observe/experience, and allow. You can also feel into your connection with the earth and all that is around you. That you are part of the "web of life" and not separate from it. You won't regret this chance to anchor yourself in the joy and tenderness that is within and around you.

1. Whether you're sitting down or moving about in your activity, take a quick *pause* to congratulate yourself for setting this time aside just for you and your well-being.

2. Find your breath and follow the flow of air passing in and out of your body. Pay attention to each breath, noticing where it goes, what it does, how it feels, when it draws in, and when it releases. Notice how each breath affects your mind and body.

3. Consider what kind of intentions you would like to set for this practice. The following intentions might work for you, or feel free to design your own intentions to fit your situation and desires. You may say aloud or to yourself: *May this practice open my heart to joy and love. May this practice foster*

a deeper awareness of the happiness all around me. May I feel supported in ways that will deepen my connection to the universe and the "web of life."

4. *Observe and experience* any and all thoughts, feelings, and sensations that rise to the surface. Without attaching a label of good or bad to each feeling, simply notice what you experience as a matter of fact, as if listing off your to-do items. You might be feeling, for example, item number one: annoyed with teenage son, check! Item number two: pissed off with coworker, check! Item number three: excited about upcoming plans with girlfriend, check! Item number four: aggravated by acidy feeling in stomach, check! And so on.

5. As you continue with your chores, remember to breathe mindfully. Each breath is an opportunity to be present and aware of your mind and body.

6. Be mindful if a happy memory, such as a recent birthday, or a smile from someone you love, or a compliment from your supervisor arises while you are doing your chores. Rest your thoughts for a moment on the feelings and sensations that this memory stirs in you, and then come back into the present moment, sweeping, washing the dishes, or whatever you are doing with mindful awareness.

7. Remember to breathe mindfully from time to time and stay in the present moment with the task at hand.

8. Gently call your attention to whatever is happening emotionally and mentally in this moment, with kindness and tenderness. *Allow* thoughts and feelings to arise, indifferent

to whether they feel good or bad, and just let them take their natural course. Feel your friends and loved ones holding space for your panic and sending you love and tenderness. Feel the earth holding space for your feelings and sending you more joy and happiness. Experience the sense of connection that you have with all beings on the planet who also long to be happy and feel loved. We are all in it together, spiraling through space, with common feelings and desires and hopes.

May your heart dwell in the joy of each moment and find love at every turn, wherever you are and whatever you're doing.

*

INTERCONNECTEDNESS

Life is full of marvelous and cherished moments. Some of those noteworthy times stick with you, while some are soon forgotten. This next practice, a version of S.T.O.P., will help anchor you in those glorious moments and strengthen your interconnectedness to the "web of life," particularly when you're drowning in a panic attack. With regular use, it will help decrease your panic and transform your life in enriching ways. Try it now.

You can do this practice sitting, standing, or lying down, at home, at work, or while running errands. If it helps, reflect on a time when you watched a sunset or sunrise. Maybe you were heading into work in the early hours of the morning and glimpsed the sun rising, casting its warm, golden light across the highway. Or maybe one evening you were in your apartment when you noticed the sun setting, splashing an amber glow on your walls and floor.

1. Take this mindful moment to stop. You are consciously taking a time-out to bring mindfulness into your mind and body and to be present, so congratulate yourself.

2. Gently put your attention on your body: the position of your arms, legs, torso, and head. Let the sensations come and go, and let your body unwind into a comfortable position. Allow any tension in your body to soften, and let go of as much tension as you can without force or pressure. Acknowledge this body of yours and its sacred bond with all of nature. Your body is grounded to the earth, which you share and inhabit with all other beings. All life is connected.

3. As your body continues to settle and unwind, purposely pay attention to the natural process and physical sensations of your breathing. Take a breath and notice where your breath is entering and leaving your body most easily. You may want to focus on the tip of your nose or on the chest or belly. Do whatever works. Bring your attention to where it's easiest to experience the sensations of your breath coming and going. Remember, you are breathing with all other breathing beings—plants, people, other animals; even the earth is breathing. And you are breathing with the earth. Feel each breath as it connects to the "web of life," all things inhaling and exhaling together.

4. Observe, acknowledge, and allow what's here right now for you. What's on your mind or in your heart? You may be thinking: *I need to call Mom. The house is a mess. I hate being late; it makes me stressed out and panicky. What if I freak out and have a meltdown in front of everyone? That would be mortifying.* Witness whatever thoughts or feelings arise. Acknowledge them and let them be. Let them come in like an unannounced guest, and watch them go out again.

5. Remember to be conscious of your breathing: in and then out, in and then out again.

6. Take this peaceful moment to recognize the self-reliance that you carry with you at all times, the ability to understand and transform your panic into greater acceptance and tenderness. You cannot stop the ocean waves, nor the waves of your panic, but you can learn to ride it out, moment by moment, breath by breath. You can learn to accept yourself

just the way that you are in this moment. You can learn to pay attention with mercy and affection.

7. Connect with your breathing again, and on your next exhale, let go of whatever thoughts and feelings or whatever old story you're attached to right now and release it, sending it outward with your breath. Make each breath count for anchoring you deeper in your awareness of the cycles of light and dark on the horizon, the highs and lows of panicky feelings, everything connected, everything evolving, everything cycling and changing.

Take this calming memory with you wherever you go, to instill a feeling of interconnectedness with this ever-spiraling, magical ball in the galaxy.

*

Supporting Your Practice

We suggest that you continue on this mindful journey, making mindfulness a way of life. You will come to undertstand that wherever you go, here you are. You can only live in the present moment, because the future has not yet happened and the past is already gone. This is your practice: to be present to whatever's happening in your life. The only moment you ever really have and live in is right now, and this is where the rubber meets the road; this is where you can make a difference in your life.

You have been introduced to a number of formal meditation practices: mindful breathing, the body scan, mindful inquiry, sitting meditation, loving-kindness meditation, and the "web of life" meditation. You are welcome to make these mindful practices your own. We recommend that you be grounded in mindful breathing as a daily practice that can help you build stability, balance, and calmness. As far as how long to meditate each day, start with short periods and build it up. Better to get five, ten, or fifteen minutes of practice in, rather than trying to do more and getting frustrated and giving up.

From time to time, practice the body scan, sitting meditation, loving-kindness meditation, or the "web of life" meditation—listen inside yourself to what feels right for you. You may also want to practice mindful inquiry as a way to explore more deeply what lies within you. No matter what practice you do, may you begin and end with some moments of loving-kindness. Whenever you make time for meditation, it's important to offer yourself kindness. It takes courage for any of us to sit and be present to ourselves amidst our ten thousand joys and sorrows.

You have also been introduced to informal practices of bringing mindfulness into your daily activities. You can be mindful while doing chores, at work, driving, brushing your teeth, washing your hands, eating, talking, or doing anything else. Make it a way of life to be mindful; of course, there will be many moments when you're not. The good news is that the moment you realize you are not present, you are! This is where the practice begins again and again. It's also important to know that there's nothing you can do about where you've been wandering, but there's everything you can do about being back in the here and now—thus the practice begins again and again.

Last, you've been introduced to other informal mindfulness practices: S.T.O.P., R.A.I.N., and "Pause, Observe/Experience, and Allow." Feel free to use the one that feels right for you in the moment. Each of these practices is an invaluable aid for managing and transforming your moments of panic and angst.

Closing Words

With the practice of mindfulness you can learn to bring your presence into the here and now, since this is where life is truly lived. In time you will grow in balance and ease with yourself and others as you lie, stand, walk, or sit. You will learn to mindfully respond to your thoughts rather than reacting to them. This will nourish your relationships with others to help both you and them grow in mutually healthy ways. So why not give it a try and see what happens when you begin to watch the show of your own stories, rather than getting so caught up in the drama? It's like being at a theater and just watching the actors. You don't need to be the star.

There's a saying in the Thai forest Buddhist tradition: If you let go a little, you'll have a little happiness; if you let go a lot, you'll have a lot of happiness; if you let go completely, you'll have complete happiness. So what would it be like to lessen your grasping and clinging? What would happen if you could begin to soar with things as they are and trust that you are not forsaken— that you will be held in the heart of this vast and mysterious universe?

As you continue to observe and allow what's within your body, emotions, and thoughts, you will gradually understand the makeup of your own mind and body and experience more freedom from panic or whatever enslaves you. You will not be so confined by a limited definition of who you think you are and will come to understand Einstein's wisdom of breaking free of this feeling that you are "separate from the rest," which he calls "a kind of optical delusion of consciousness" (*New York Post*, November 28, 1972).

Through the "web of life" and loving-kindness practices you will begin to feel more connected to yourself, to the people around you, to the natural world, and to the universe. As your experience of interconnection grows, you'll also find more purpose in life and have more participation and engagement with it.

Achaan Chah (1985, 162), a wise Thai forest Buddhist meditation master, points the way to this discovery by inviting us to sit back and watch the workings of our mind and body so that we grow in deep understanding and wisdom.

> Try to be mindful, and let things take their natural course. Then your mind will become still in any surroundings, like a still forest pool. All kinds of wonderful, rare animals will come to drink at the pool, and you will clearly see the nature of all things. You will see many strange and wonderful things come and go, but you will be still. This is the happiness of the Buddha.

May we also remember that meditation is an act of love, a journey of befriending ourselves, others, and the world. Bob Sharples (2003, 18), an Australian meditation teacher, says this so eloquently:

> Don't meditate to fix yourself, to heal yourself, to improve yourself, to redeem yourself; rather, do it as an act of love, of deep warm friendship to yourself. In this

way there is no longer any need for the subtle aggression of self-improvement, for the endless guilt of not doing enough. It offers the possibility of an end to the ceaseless round of trying so hard that wraps so many people's lives in a knot. Instead there is now meditation as an act of love. How endlessly delightful and encouraging.

As you grow in mindfulness, you will become more settled with yourself, others, and the world. We would like to offer this last, beautiful poem to you, by Wendell Berry, "The Peace of Wild Things" (1998), which speaks of this safety and ease and the interconnectedness of life.

When despair for the world grows in me
and I wake in the night at the least sound,
in fear of what my life and my children's life may be,

I go and lie down where the wood drake
rests in his beauty on the water,
and the great heron feeds.

I come into the peace of wild things
who do not tax their lives
with forethought of grief.

I come into the presence of still water.
And I feel above me the day-blind stars
waiting with their light. For a time
I rest in the grace of the world, and am free.

Resources

Mindfulness Meditation Audio CDs by Bob Stahl, PhD

To purchase or listen to a sample of the following CDs, visit mindfulnessprograms.com/mindful-healing-series. You can also purchase all except the last three at Amazon.com. All CDs published by Bob Stahl, PhD, in 2005.

Opening to Change, Forgiveness, and Loving-Kindness

Working with Chronic Pain

Working with Neck and Shoulder Pain

Working with Back Pain

Working with Insomnia and Sleep Challenges

Working with Anxiety, Fear, and Panic

Working with High Blood Pressure

Working with Heart Disease

Working with Headaches and Migraines

Working with Asthma, COPD, and Respiratory Challenges

Body Scan and Sitting Meditation

Lying and Standing Yoga

Impermanence and Loving-Kindness Meditation

DVD by Bob Stahl, PhD

Mindful Qigong and Loving-Kindness Meditation (available at mindfulnessprograms.com/mindful-healing-series). 2007.

Books by Bob Stahl, PhD

A Mindfulness-Based Stress Reduction Workbook (co-authored with Elisha Goldstein, PhD). Oakland, CA: New Harbinger Publications, 2010.

Living with Your Heart Wide Open: How Mindfulness and Compassion Can Free You from Unworthiness, Inadequacy, and Shame (co-authored with Steve Flowers, MFT). Oakland, CA: New Harbinger Publications, 2011.

Mindfulness-Based Stress Reduction Programs

Mindfulness-based stress reduction programs abound throughout the United States as well as internationally. If you're interested in joining a program near you, check out the regional and international directory at the Center for Mindfulness at the University of Massachusetts Medical School's website: http://w3.umassmed.edu/MBSR/public/searchmember.aspx.

Mindfulness Books

Analayo, B. 2002. *Satipatthana: The Direct Path to Realization.* Birmingham, UK: Windhorse Publications.

Boorstein, S. 1997. *It's Easier Than You Think: The Buddhist Way to Happiness.* San Francisco: HarperOne.

Brach, T. 2003. *Radical Acceptance: Embracing Your Life with the Heart of a Buddha.* New York: Bantam.

———. 2013 *True Refuge: Finding Peace and Freedom in Your Own Awakened Heart.* New York: Bantam.

Brantley, J. 2007. *Calming Your Anxious Mind: How Mindfulness and Compassion Can Free You from Anxiety, Fear, and Panic.* Oakland, CA: New Harbinger Publications.

Chödrön, P. 2000. *When Things Fall Apart: Heart Advice for Difficult Times.* Boston: Shambhala.

———. 2007. *The Places That Scare You: A Guide to Fearlessness in Difficult Times.* Boston: Shambhala.

Dass, R., and S. Levine. 1988. *Grist for the Mill.* Berkeley, CA: Celestial Arts.

Epstein, M. 1995. *Thoughts without a Thinker: Psychotherapy from a Buddhist Perspective.* New York: Basic.

Flowers, S. 2009. *The Mindful Path through Shyness: How Mindfulness and Compassion Can Help Free You from Social Anxiety, Fear, and Avoidance.* Oakland, CA: New Harbinger Publications.

Flowers, S, and B. Stahl. 2011. *Living With Your Heart Wide Open: How Mindfulness and Compassion Can Free You from Unworthiness, Inadequacy, and Shame.* Oakland, CA: New Harbinger Publications.

Goldstein, J. 1983. *The Experience of Insight: A Simple and Direct Guide to Buddhist Meditation.* Boston: Shambhala.

————. 2003. *Insight Meditation: The Practice of Freedom.* Boston: Shambhala.

————. 2003. *One Dharma: The Emerging Western Buddhism.* San Francisco: Harper.

Goldstein, J., and J. Kornfield. 2001. *Seeking the Heart of Wisdom: The Path of Insight Meditation.* Boston: Shambhala.

Gunaratana, B. H. 2002. *Mindfulness in Plain English.* Boston: Wisdom Publications.

Hanson, R., and R. Mendius. 2009. *Buddha's Brain: The Practical Neuroscience of Happiness, Love, and Wisdom.* Oakland, CA: New Harbinger Publications.

Kabat-Zinn, J. 1990. *Full Catastrophe Living: Using the Wisdom of Your Body and Mind to Face Stress, Pain, and Illness.* New York: Delta.

————. 1994. *Wherever You Go, There You Are: Mindfulness Meditation in Everyday Life.* New York: Hyperion.

————. 2005. *Coming to Our Senses: Healing Ourselves and the World through Mindfulness.* New York: Hyperion.

————. 2012. *Mindfulness for Beginners: Reclaiming the Present Moment—and Your Life.* Boulder: Sounds True.

Kornfield, J. 1993. *A Path with Heart: A Guide through the Perils and Promises of Spiritual Life.* New York: Bantam.

————. 2000. *After the Ecstasy, the Laundry: How the Heart Grows Wise on the Spiritual Path.* New York: Bantam.

————. 2008. *The Wise Heart: A Guide to the Universal Teachings of Buddhist Psychology.* New York: Bantam.

Levine, N. 2003. *Dharma Punx: A Memoir.* San Francisco: HarperCollins.

————. 2007. *Against the Stream: A Buddhist Manual for Spiritual Revolutionaries.* San Francisco: HarperCollins.

Levine, S. 1989. *A Gradual Awakening.* 2nd ed. New York: Anchor.

Rosenberg, L. 1998. *Breath by Breath: The Liberating Practice of Insight Meditation.* Boston: Shambhala.

———. 2000. *Living in the Light of Death: On the Art of Being Truly Alive.* Boston: Shambhala.

Salzberg, S. 1997. *A Heart as Wide as the World: Stories on the Path of Lovingkindness.* Boston: Shambhala.

———. 2002. *Lovingkindness: The Revolutionary Art of Happiness.* Boston: Shambhala.

Santorelli, S. 1999. *Heal Thyself: Lessons in Mindfulness in Medicine.* New York: Three Rivers Press.

Segal, Z., M. Williams, and J. Teasdale. 2002. *Mindfulness-Based Cognitive Therapy for Depression: A New Approach to Preventing Relapse.* New York: Guilford Press.

Siegel, D. 2007. *The Mindful Brain: Reflection and Attunement in the Cultivation of Well-Being.* New York: W. W. Norton.

Stahl, B., and E. Goldstein. 2010. *A Mindfulness-Based Stress Reduction Workbook.* Oakland, CA: New Harbinger Publications.

Thera, Nyanaponika. 1973. *The Heart of Buddhist Meditation.* Boston: Weiser Books.

Thich Nhat Hanh. 1996. *The Miracle of Mindfulness.* Boston: Beacon.

———. 2005. *Being Peace.* Berkeley, CA: Parallax Press.

Books to Move You into the Heart

Berry, W. 1998. *The Selected Poems of Wendell Berry.* Berkeley, CA: Counterpoint Press.

Faulds, D. 2002. *Go In and In.* Kearney, NE. Morris Press.

Hafiz. 1999. *The Gift*. Translated by D. Ladinski. New York: Penguin.

Kabir. 2004. *Kabir: Ecstatic Poems*. Translated by R. Bly. Boston: Beacon.

Lao-tzu. 1944. *The Way of Life*. Translated by W. Bynner. New York: Penguin.

Oliver, M. 1992. *New and Selected Poems*. Boston: Beacon Books.

Rumi. 2001. *The Soul of Rumi*. Translated by C. Barks. San Francisco: Harper.

Ryokan. 1977. *One Robe, One Bowl*. Translated by J. Stevens. New York: John Weatherhill.

Stafford, W. 1998. *The Way It Is*. St. Paul, MN: Graywolf Press.

Walcott, D. 1987. *Collected Poems*. New York: Farrar, Straus and Giroux.

Welwood, J. P. 1998. *Poems for the Path*. Mill Valley, CA: Author.

Whyte, D. 1994. *The Heart Aroused*. New York: Bantam Doubleday.

Meditation Timers

You can download free meditation timers from the Insight Meditation Center at http://www.insightmeditationcenter.org/meditation-timers/.

References

Berry, W. 1998. "The Peace of Wild Things." In *The Selected Poems of Wendell Berry*. Berkeley, CA: Counterpoint Press.

Center for Mindfulness in Medicine, Health Care, and Society. N.d. "Major Research Findings." http://www.umassmed.edu/Content.aspx?id=42426.

Chah, Achaan. 1985. *A Still Forest Pool: The Insight Meditation of Achaan Chah*. Compiled by J. Kornfield and P. Breiter. Wheaton, IL: Quest.

Covey, S. 2008. Foreword to *Prisoners of Our Thoughts: Viktor Frankl's Principles for Discovering Meaning in Life and Work*, by A. Pattakos. San Francisco: Berrett-Koehler.

Davidson, R. J., J. Kabat-Zinn, J. Schumacher, M. Rosenkranz, D. Muller, S. F. Santorelli, F. Urbanowski, A. Harrington, K. Bonus, and J. F. Sheridan. 2003. "Alterations in Brain and Immune Function Produced by Mindfulness Meditation." *Psychosomatic Medicine* 65 (4): 564–570.

Faulds, D. 2002. "Allow." In *Go In and In*. Kearney, NE: Morris Press.

Hölzel, B. K., J. Carmody, M. Vangel, C. Congleton, S. M. Yerramsetti, T. Gard, and S. Lazar. 2011. "Mindfulness Practice Leads to Increases in Regional Brain Gray Matter Density." *Psychiatry Research: Neuroimaging* 191 (1): 36–43.

Lao-tzu. 1944. *The Way of Life.* Translated by W. Bynner. New York: Penguin.

Miller, J., K. Fletcher, and J. Kabat-Zinn. 1993. "Three-Year Follow-Up and Clinical Implications of a Mindfulness-Based Stress Reduction Intervention in the Treatment of Anxiety Disorders." *Gen. Hosp. Psychiatry* 17: 192–200.

Sharples, B. 2003. *Meditation: Calming the Mind.* Melbourne, Australia: Lothian.

Welwood, J. P. 1998. "Unconditional." In *Poems for the Path.* Mill Valley, CA: Author.

Bob Stahl, PhD, is the founder and director of the mindfulness-based stress reduction programs at Dominican Hospital, O'Connor Hospital, and El Camino Hospital. Bob serves as a senior teacher for Oasis, an institute for mindfulness-based professional education and innovation. Bob is the guiding teacher at Insight Santa Cruz and visiting teacher at Spirit Rock and Insight Meditation Society. He is coauthor of *Living with Your Heart Wide Open* and the *Mindfulness-Based Stress Reduction Workbook*. Stahl lives in Santa Cruz, CA.

Wendy Millstine, is a freelance writer and certified holistic nutrition consultant who specializes in diet and stress reduction. With Jeffrey Brantley, she is coauthor of the *Five Good Minutes*® series, and *Daily Meditations for Calming Your Anxious Mind*. She is also coauthor of *True Belonging*. She lives in Santa Rosa, CA.

MORE BOOKS *from*
NEW HARBINGER PUBLICATIONS

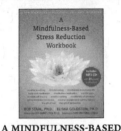

A MINDFULNESS-BASED STRESS REDUCTION WORKBOOK

US $24.95 / ISBN: 978-1572247086
Also available as an e-book at newharbinger.com

FIVE GOOD MINUTES®

100 Morning Practices to Help You Stay Calm & Focused All Day Long

US $14.95 / ISBN: 978-1572244146
Also available as an e-book at newharbinger.com

THIRTY-MINUTE THERAPY FOR ANXIETY

Everything You Need to Know in the Least Amount of Time

US $15.95 / ISBN: 978-1572249813
Also available as an e-book at newharbinger.com

THE STRESS RESPONSE

How Dialectical Behavior Therapy Can Free You from Needless Anxiety, Worry, Anger & Other Symptoms of Stress

US $17.95 / ISBN: 978-1608821303
Also available as an e-book at newharbinger.com

THE ANXIETY & PHOBIA WORKBOOK, FIFTH EDITION

US $24.95 / ISBN: 978-1572248915
Also available as an e-book at newharbinger.com

THE DAILY RELAXER

Relax Your Body, Calm Your Mind & Refresh Your Spirit

US $14.95 / ISBN: 978-1572244542
Also available as an e-book at newharbinger.com

new*harbinger*publications, inc.
1-800-748-6273 / newharbinger.com

(VISA, MC, AMEX / prices subject to change without notice)

Like us on Facebook

Follow us on Twitter
@newharbinger.com

 Don't miss out on new books in the subjects that interest you.
Sign up for our **Book Alerts** at nhpubs.com/bookalerts

Check out www.psychsolve.com

Psych*Solve*® offers help with diagnosis, including treatment information on mental health issues, such as depression, bipolar disorder, anxiety, phobias, stress and trauma, relationship problems, eating disorders, chronic pain, and many other disorders.